True Bear Stories
by Joaquin Miller

with a foreword by William Everson
and woodblocks by Vincent Perez

Edited by James Robertson

CAPRA PRESS
SANTA BARBARA
1987

This little collection of wild animal stories describes a California
and a way of life that exists today only in memory. There lies its charm
and its usefulness. As originally issued, *True Bear Stories* included
some material which described neither place nor time and for that
reason has been left out of the present edition. For the most part,
those portions were peripheral to the author's purpose and were
written by others. The principal exception is a California Indian
creation tale, retold by Miller, which we have omitted because it is a
bear of quite another color, being more legend than description of an
actual encounter between human and animal.

This Capra edition is a photo offset reprinting of the limited edition
originally issued in 1985 by The Yolla Bolly Press as a part of their
California Writers of the Land series.

LIBRARY OF CONGRESS CATALOGING-IN-PUBLICATION DATA
Miller, Joaquin, 1837–1913.
True bear stories.
1. Bears—California.   I. Robertson, James, 1935–
II. Title.
QL795.B4M6 1987   599.74'446'09794   86-31688
ISBN 0-88496-259-8

CAPRA PRESS
Post Office Box 2068
Santa Barbara, California 93120

TABLE OF CONTENTS

Pondering the life of Joaquin Miller in the light of this book, one of his last publications, I became aware of a symbolic affinity between him and the Golden Bear of California—something to do with the end of an era. Miller died in 1913, just nine years before the last "yellowtip" was slain on Horse Corral Meadow in Fresno County. In a sense they were both anachronisms, out of phase with this century, and therefore dismissable as irrelevant. On the other hand their irrelevance to the opening of the century makes them relevant to its close. The break with the past was so rapidly effected that now, in our search for roots, they regain significance.

In its day the California grizzly was unquestionably the most formidable beast on the American continent. Larger and stronger than the "silvertip" of the Rockies, it was dubbed "yellowtip" by the mountain men, a sobriquet that evolved into the Golden Bear of our State Emblem.

It is difficult to grasp the impact of this animal on the consciousness of its time. Until the arrival of the Spaniards the grizzly held the numerous Indian tribes in absolute terror. Competing for the same food resources, which ranged from roots and acorns to stranded whales, they intersected at the tension point of survival. The first Franciscan missionaries wrote of the appalling scarification of many Indians attacked by bears. Even after the secularization of the missions and the expansion of the great ranchos that made up the colorful "California Pastoral" period preceding the Bear Flag takeover, the grizzlies lived pretty much as they wanted to, as they always had and always expected to. In fact they underwent a population explosion due to the surplus of meat discarded from cattle grown solely for hides exportable to the Atlantic Seaboard and Europe. In *Two Years Before the Mast*, Dana's brig *Pilgrim* took home 40,000 hides representing untold tons of wasted beef. And that was just one ship. Picture in your mind the ungodly ferocity of scores of grizzlies snarling and fighting day and night in the stench of the killing grounds.

But with the coming of the Yankees and their long rifles the tables were turned, and after the Gold Rush the grizzlies went into a rapid decline. Yet even then it was not the rifle alone that finally exterminated them; there was also the strychnine scattered by sheep ranchers who, each summer, after the Central Valley burned dry under the raging sun, sent their flocks into the high Sierras, following the receding greenery right up to the snow line. John Muir, in the diary he kept on his first trek into the mountains, wrote of the unequal contest between terrified sheepherders and the awesome grizzlies that had acquired a taste for mutton. But by the time Joaquin Miller brought out his little book of bear stories in 1900 the grizzly tribe was virtually extinct, and he knew it. Therefore his book carries a breath of nostalgia, the aura of a mighty race that soon would be no more.

In my book *Archetype West* I hailed Joaquin Miller as the inceptor of the western literary archetype, its autochthon. Alan Rosenus, to whom we owe the rescue of the poet from his latter-day oblivion, holds that he retained the vitality of his prose to the end of his life, pointing to *Overland in a Covered Wagon* and *True Bear Stories* as evidence. Presented by a reputable New York publisher the bear stories immediately went through several printings, then settled down to a long life. In fact it was kept in print well beyond the mid-century mark, emerging as Miller's most successful volume, gaining for itself something of the status of a popular American classic, a staple of the outdoors boy's bookshelf, between the Scout's Manual and Seton's *Wild Animals I Have Known*.

But as originally issued the book is something of an anomaly. Ostensibly a children's book, it smacks of a text pulled together in a publisher's office by editorial caprice or publicational opportunism. The first book Miller published after his ill-fated trek to the Klondike gold rush of 1897–98, he more than likely found himself strapped for money and sought a quick way to recover his losses via the juvenile book market. The work is dedicated to his daughter Juanita, and he acknowledged she inspired it, but in the text he mostly responds to his readership as "boys." The writing seems leisurely and unforced, suggesting he had picked it up now and then in his spare time, to abruptly cut it off unfinished when the prospect of publication beckoned, hastily padding it out with extraneous features. In a word, he subverted the focus of the book's original conception in an attempt to appeal to the general reader.

What are these extraneous features? They include Introductory Notes by David Starr Jordan, president of Stanford University; a reprinting of a long account, not written by Miller, of how the grizzly "Monarch" was captured and carried to the San Francisco zoo, an account lifted from the *San Francisco Examiner* of the previous decade; and finally a pretentiously entitled essay, "The Scientific Classification of Bears," author unspecified, but "edited" by one Pierre W. Berenger, a work so much an afterthought it isn't even included in the Table of Contents! Of these three features the most interesting is that of David Starr Jordan, not so much for what he wrote as for his very presence in the book.

For Jordan was a personal friend, and it is just possible that his inclusion here was dictated by editorial circumspection. Miller still carried the onus of his passionate championship of the beleaguered Indian tribes of Northern California, beset by a horde of ruthless claim-jumpers backed by the U.S. Army. In *Life Amongst the Modocs* Miller rebuked his fellow citizens. Completed and first published in London it became a critical and polemical success, thus infuriating the Indian-lynchers in his own country, who cursed him for a fraud, pointing out that his actual experience was confined to the Shasta and Pitt River tribes, and not the Modocs at all.

The charge was technically true enough, but at the same time was patently diversionary. The Shastas and the Modocs, though enemies, were approximate peoples, lived the same lifestyle, and were in mutually desperate straits. Everything Miller wrote about the Shastas applied with equal force to the Modocs, save the latter had a superior redoubt in the lava beds, could hold out longer and hence command greater media attention. Thus the Modocs became a liberal *cause celebre* and provided too good an opportunity to let a few miles between tribes stand in the way of a stunning polemical *tour de force*. So life amongst the Shastas became life amongst the Modocs, with Miller reviled for a fraud. Given the indictment, the collaboration of the prestigious university's president counted for something. Unfortunately, taken with the other two appendages, it also compromised the aesthetic unity of the book.

Not only so, but that presence impugns the credibility of the stories by laying claim to an objectivity they actually do not possess, a matter largely responsible for the book's descent into oblivion. When Storrer and Tevis in their definitive *California Grizzly* dismiss *True Bear Stories* as "erroneous in title and content," they speak as professional biologists. But aesthetic form is not so rigid: the truth of the poet subsumes the truth of the scientist. Expunge the offending material and another dimension emerges. We leave the domain of fact and enter the domain of desire, the magic realm of myth.

The relevance of the present edition, then, is that it gives us Miller in his spontaneity and freshness unencumbered by pseudo-scientific and journalistic trappings. In effect it places him where he belongs, in the company of his famous compeers, Bret Harte and Mark Twain. Can he sustain the comparison? In *Life Amongst the Modocs*, his masterpiece, he could and did. Indeed, his moral and spiritual intensity, born of the anguish of involvement, places him above them. But here in these bear stories, his purpose is to entertain. In this he is closer to the autobiographical anecdotes of Twain, though he can't approach the latter's savage irony and side-splitting gusto.

Nevertheless, these stories, as reminiscences, as *experience*, survive. For the verisimilitude of direct personal involvement is bodied forth in a singular offhand but infectious style, an artless beguilement, subsuming the element of wonder intrinsic to childhood, an element sourced in unpremeditated affinity rather than cultivated emotion. Take this passage from "Music-Loving Bears." Forty years earlier Miller as a boy accompanied his father and a man named Lyte Howard on an overnight trip to haul, by oxcart, a load of grain to the mill. They camped by a river, and around the campfire Lyte, a fiddler, struck up a tune. As the night wore on, three bears, unbeknownst to them, but compelled by the music, silently approached.

Then suddenly father seemed to feel the presence of something or someone strange, and I felt it, too. But the fiddler felt, heard, saw nothing but the divine, wild melody that made the very pine trees dance and quiver to their tips. Oh, for the pure, wild, sweet, plaintive music once more! the music of "Money Musk," "Zip Coon," "Ol' Dan Tucker," and all the other dear old airs that once made a thousand happy feet keep time on the puncheon floors from Hudson's bank to the Oregon. But they are no more, now. They have passed away forever with the Indian, the pioneer, and the music-loving bear. It is strange how a man—I mean the natural man—will feel a presence long before he hears it or sees it. You can always feel the approach of a—but I forget. You are of another generation, a generation that only reads, takes thought at second hand only, if at all, and you would not understand; so let us get forward and not waste time in explaining the unexplainable to you.

Now this artlessness, this beguilement, is due not only to the writer's creative naiveté, his subliminal innocence, but also to the subject under regard, in this case the bear. For the unconscious affinity between man and bear is powerful. Miller himself speaks of it almost as a matter of temperament, though both Indians and mountain men were struck by the physical resemblance to the human form when a bear was skinned out and hung up for quartering. But Thomas MacNamee, in his impressive book *The Grizzly Bear*, points to the biological situation that each species shares a sovereign place at the top of its food chain, endowing each with a marked deficiency in the fugitive virtues of timorousness and covert circumspection. We live like lords of the earth, and like lords we dispute.

Then, too, symbolically the bear embodies both maternal and paternal attributes. The maternal characteristics are endowed in the bear's cave-dwelling habits, its annual hibernation, and its female devotion to its young; in the latter it surpasses the human mother. Thus it serves in the rites of passage practiced by most aboriginal peoples, when the pubescent youth pass from the domain of the mother to that of the father, invoking the bear as a protective spirit. The masculine aspect emerges as symbolic presence further along in the ongoing rites that represent psychic evolution —the spiritual or demonic aspect of the bear in the sharing of the sacred totem as sacrificial meal, representing, as Joseph Henderson in his *Rites of Initiation* observes: "the prestige and ultimate power of the animal master, ancestor of the race, his crown of consciousness and his burning inner soul, made manifest through his eyes, the image of godhead."

I cite these symbolic attributes in order to give some indication of the power of the bear across the span of human existence, its ability to command our fascination over uncounted centuries. That the fascination still exists can hardly be doubted. Everyone has some notion of what is meant by one's totem animal, and I dare say the bear is the most extensively adopted of them all—the identification is that close. In my own case the bear emerged very early in my life when, as a child, on being shown the man in the moon, I could only distinguish a bear, a fact which remains true to this day. On the basis of this singularity I took for my occult or aboriginal name: Moon Bear.

Since I have injected my personal experience into this account let me close with an anecdote: When first approached to do this Foreword I hesitated. I was interested in both bears and Joaquin Miller, but was unsure of how to preside over their long love affair, and besides, I was put off by the nominal juvenile attribution. Still, I began to leaf through the pages, sampling passages here and there. Suddenly my heart jumped. Out of the paragraph before me sprang an electrifying admonition: "Never run uphill from a bear!" I was swept back sixty years to my own boyhood. A book on bears had come to my hand in the public library of Selma, the California town in which I grew up. It must have been just about the time the last "yellowtip" was put to sleep on Horse Corral Meadow. Over the years I had forgotten title and author, but one fragment stayed with me, like a splinter of light in a mountain of mist. Now it hit me: *"Never run uphill from a bear!"* The very book! Tipping my hat to the spirit of Joaquin Miller I took up my pen. I had come full circle.

WILLIAM EVERSON

February 11, 1985
Kingfisher Flat
Davenport, California

TRUE BEAR STORIES

I

IT IS NOW more than a quarter of a century since I saw
the woods of Mount Shasta in flames, and beasts of all
sorts, even serpents, crowded together; but I can never forget, never!

It looked as if we would have a cloudburst that fearful
morning. We three were making our way by slow marches
from Soda Springs across the south base of Mount Shasta
to the Modoc lava beds—two English artists and myself.
We had saddle horses, or, rather, two saddle horses and a
mule, for our own use. Six Indians, with broad leather or
elkskin straps across their foreheads, had been chartered to
carry the kits and traps. They were men of means and lei-
sure, these artists, and were making the trip for the fish,
game, scenery and excitement and everything, in fact, that
was in the adventure. I was merely their hired guide.

This second morning out, the Indians—poor slaves, perhaps, from the first, certainly not warriors with any spirit
in them—began to sulk. They had risen early and kept
hovering together and talking, or, rather, making signs in
the gloomiest sort of fashion. We had hard work to get them
to do anything at all, and even after breakfast was ready
they packed up without tasting food.

The air was ugly, for that region—hot, heavy, and without light or life. It was what in some parts of South America
they call "earthquake weather." Even the horses sulked as
we mounted; but the mule shot ahead through the brush at
once, and this induced the ponies to follow.

The Englishmen thought the Indians and horses were
only tired from the day before, but we soon found the whole

1

force plowing ahead through the dense brush and over fallen timber on a double quick.

Then we heard low, heavy thunder in the heavens. Were they running away from a thunderstorm? The English artists, who had been doing India and had come to love the indolent patience and obedience of the black people, tried to call a halt. No use. I shouted to the Indians in their own tongue. "Tokau! Ki-sa! Kiu!" (Hasten! Quick! Quick!) was all the answer I could get from the red, hot face that was thrown for a moment back over the load and shoulder. So we shot forward. In fact, the horses now refused all regard for the bit, and made their own way through the brush with wondrous skill and speed.

We were flying from fire, not flood! Pitiful what a few years of neglect will do toward destroying a forest! When a lad I had galloped my horse in security and comfort all through this region. It was like a park then. Now it was a dense tangle of undergrowth and a mass of fallen timber. What a feast for flames! In one of the very old books on America in the British Museum—possibly the very oldest on the subject—the author tells of the parklike appearance of the American forests. He tells his English friends back at home that it is most comfortable to ride to the hounds, "since the Indian squats (squaws) do set fire to the brush and leaves every spring."

But the "squats" had long since disappeared from the forests of Mount Shasta; and here we were tumbling over and tearing through ten years' or more of accumulation of logs, brush, leaves, weeds and grass that lay waiting for a sea of fire to roll over all like a mass of lava.

And now the wind blew past and over us. Bits of white ashes sifted down like snow. Surely the sea of fire was coming, coming right on after us! Still there was no sign, save this little sift of ashes, no sound; nothing at all except the trained sense of the Indians and the terror of the "cattle" (this is what the Englishmen called our horses) to give us warning. In a short time we struck an arroyo, or canyon, that was nearly free from brush and led steeply down to the cool and deep waters of the McCloud River. Here we found the Indians had thrown their loads and themselves on the ground.

They got up in sulky silence, and, stripping our horses, turned them loose; and then, taking our saddles, they led us hastily up out of the narrow mouth of the arroyo under a little steep stone bluff.

They did not say a word or make any sign, and we were all too breathless and bewildered to either question or protest. The sky was black, and thunder made the woods tremble. We were hardly done wiping the blood and perspiration from our torn hands and faces where we sat when the mule jerked up his head, sniffed, snorted and then plunged headlong into the river and struck out for the deep forest on the farther bank, followed by the ponies.

The mule is the most traduced of all animals. A single mule has more sense than a whole stableful of horses. You can handle a mule easily if the barn is burning; he keeps his head; but a horse becomes insane. He will rush right into the fire, if allowed to, and you can only handle him, and that with difficulty if he sniffs the fire, by blindfolding him. Trust a mule in case of peril or a panic long before a horse. The brother of Solomon and willful son of David surely had some of the great temple-builder's wisdom and discernment, for we read that he rode a mule. True, he lost his head and got hung up by the hair, but that is nothing against the mule.

As we turned our eyes from seeing the animals safely over, right there by us and a little behind us, through the willows of the canyon and over the edge of the water, we saw peering and pointing toward the other side dozens of long black and brown outreaching noses. Elk!

They had come noiselessly, they stood motionless. They

3

did not look back or aside, only straight ahead. We could almost have touched the nearest one. They were large and fat, almost as fat as cows; certainly larger than the ordinary Jersey. The peculiar thing about them was the way, the level way, in which they held their small, long heads— straight out; the huge horns of the males lying far back on their shoulders. And then for the first time I could make out what these horns are for— to part the brush with as they lead through the thicket, and thus save their coarse coats of hair, which is very rotten, and could be torn off in a little time if not thus protected. They are never used to fight with, never; the elk uses only his feet. If on the defense, however, the male elk will throw his nose close to the ground and receive the enemy on his horns.

Suddenly and all together, and perhaps they had only paused a second, they moved on into the water, led by a bull with a head of horns like a rockingchair. And his rocking-chair rocked his head under water much of the time. The cold, swift water soon broke the line, only the leader making the bank directly before us, while the others drifted far down and out of sight.

Our artists, meantime, had dug up pencil and pad and begun work. But an Indian jerked the saddles, on which the Englishmen sat, aside, and the work was stopped. Everything was now packed up close under the steep little ledge of rocks. An avalanche of smaller wild animals, mostly deer, was upon us. Many of these had their tongues hanging from their half-opened mouths. They did not attempt to drink, as you would suppose, but slid into the water silently almost as soon as they came. Surely they must have seen us, but certainly they took no notice of us. And such order! No crushing or crowding, as you see cattle in corrals, aye, as you see people sometimes in the cars.

And now came a torrent of little creeping things: rabbits, rats, squirrels! None of these smaller creatures attempted

4

to cross, but crept along in the willows and brush close to the water. They loaded down the willows till they bent into the water, and the terrified little creatures floated away without the least bit of noise or confusion. And still the black skies were filled with the solemn boom of thunder. In fact, we had not yet heard any noise of any sort except thunder, not even our own voices. There was something more eloquent in the air now, something more terrible than man or beast, and all things were awed into silence — a profound silence.

And all this time countless creatures, little creatures and big, were crowding the bank on our side or swimming across or floating down, down, down the swift, wood-hung waters. Suddenly the stolid leader of the Indians threw his two naked arms in the air and let them fall, limp and helpless at his side; then he pointed out into the stream, for there embers and living and dead beasts began to drift and sweep down the swift waters from above. The Indians now gathered up the packs and saddles and made a barricade above, for it was clear that many a living thing would now be borne down upon us.

The two Englishmen looked one another in the face long and thoughtfully, pulling their feet under them to keep from being trodden on. Then, after another avalanche of creatures of all sorts and sizes, a sort of Noah's ark this time, one of them said to the other:

"Beastly, you know!"

"Awful beastly, don't you know!"

As they were talking entirely to themselves and in their own language, I did not trouble myself to call their attention to an enormous yellow rattlesnake which had suddenly and noiselessly slid down, over the steep little bluff of rocks behind us, into our midst.

But now note this fact—every man there, red or white, saw or felt that huge and noiseless monster the very second she slid among us. For as I looked, even as I first looked, and then turned to see what the others would do, they were all looking at the glittering eyes set in that coffinlike head.

The Indians did not move back or seem nearly so much frightened as when they saw the drift of embers and dead beasts in the river before them; but the florid Englishmen turned white! They resolutely arose, thrust their hands in their pockets and stood leaning their backs hard against the steep bluff. Then another snake, long, black and beautiful, swept his supple neck down between them and thrust his red tongue forth—as if a bit of the flames had already reached us.

Fortunately, this particular "wisest of all the beasts of the field," was not disposed to tarry. In another second he had swung to the ground and was making a thousand graceful curves in the swift water for the further bank.

The world, even the world of books, seems to know nothing at all about the wonderful snakes that live in the woods. The woods rattlesnake is as large as at least twenty ordinary rattlesnakes; and Indians say it is entirely harmless. The enormous black snake, I know, is entirely without venom. In all my life, spent mostly in the camp, I have seen only three of those monstrous yellow woods rattlesnakes; one in Indiana, one in Oregon and the other on this occasion here on the banks of the McCloud. Such bright eyes! It was hard to stop looking at them.

Meantime a good many bears had come and gone. The bear is a good swimmer, and takes to the water without fear. He is, in truth, quite a fisherman; so much of a fisherman, in fact, that in salmon season here his flesh is unfit for food. The pitiful part of it all was to see such little creatures as could not swim clinging all up and down and not daring to take to the water.

Unlike his domesticated brother, we saw several wildcats take to the water promptly. The wildcat, you must know,

*Over our heads like a rocket leaped a huge
black bear, a ball of fire!*

has no tail to speak of. But the panther and Californian lion are well equipped in this respect and abhor the water.

I constantly kept an eye over my shoulder at the ledge or little bluff of rocks, expecting to see a whole row of lions and panthers sitting there, almost "cheek by jowl" with my English friends, at any moment. But strangely enough, we saw neither panther nor lion; nor did we see a single grizzly among all the bears that came that way.

We now noticed that one of the Indians had become fascinated or charmed by looking too intently at the enormous serpent in our midst. The snake's huge, coffin-shaped head, as big as your open palm, was slowly swaying from side to side. The Indian's head was doing the same, and their eyes were drawing closer and closer together. Whatever there may be in the Bible story of Eve and the serpent, whether a figure or a fact, who shall say?—but it is certainly, in some sense, true.

An Indian will not kill a rattlesnake. But to break the charm, in this case, they caught their companion by the shoulders and forced him back flat on the ground. And there he lay, crying like a child, the first and only Indian I ever saw cry. And then suddenly boom! boom! boom! as if heaven burst. It began to rain in torrents.

And just then, as we began to breathe freely and feel safe, there came a crash and bump and bang above our heads, and high over our heads from off the ledge behind us! Over our heads like a rocket, in an instant and clear into the water, leaped a huge black bear, a ball of fire! his fat sides in flame. He sank out of sight but soon came up, spun around like a top, dived again, then again spun around. But he got across, I am glad to say. And this always pleases my little girl, Juanita. He sat there on the bank looking back at us quite a time. Finally he washed his face, like a cat, then quietly went away. The rattlesnake was the last to cross.

The beautiful yellow beast was not at all disconcerted,

but with the serenest dignity lifted her yellow folds, coiled and uncoiled slowly, curved high in the air, arched her glittering neck of gold, widened her body till broad as your two hands, and so slid away over the water to the other side through the wild white rain. The cloudburst put out the fire instantly, showing that, though animals have superhuman foresight, they don't know everything before the time.

"Beastly! I didn't get a blawsted sketch, you know."

"Awful beastly! Neither did I, don't you know."

And that was all my English friends said. The Indians made their moaning and whimpering friend who had been overcome by the snake pull himself together and they swam across and gathered up the "cattle."

Some men say a bear cannot leap; but I say there are times when a bear can leap like a tiger. This was one of those times.

II

MUSIC-LOVING BEARS

NO, DON'T DESPISE the bear, either in his life or his death. He is a kingly fellow, every inch a king; a curious, monkish, music-loving, roving Robin Hood of his somber woods—a silent monk, who knows a great deal more than he tells. And please don't go to look at him and sit in judgment on him behind the bars. Put yourself in his place and see how much of manhood or kinghood would be left in you with a muzzle on your mouth, and only enough liberty left to push your nose between two rusty bars and catch the peanut which the little boy has found to be a bad one and so generously tosses it to the bear.

Of course, the little boy, remembering the experience of about forty other little boys in connection with the late baldheaded Elijah, has a prejudice against the bear family,

10

but why the full-grown man should so continually persist in caging this shaggy-coated, dignified, kingly and ancient brother of his, I cannot see, unless it is that he knows almost nothing at all of his better nature, his shy, innocent love of a joke, his partiality for music and his imperial disdain of death. And so, with a desire that man may know a little more about this storied and classic creature which, with noiseless and stately tread, has come down to us out of the past, and is as quietly passing away from the face of the earth, these fragmentary facts are set down. But first as to his love of music. A bear loves music better than he loves honey, and that is saying that he loves music better than he loves his life.

We were going to mill, father and I, and Lyte Howard, in Oregon, about forty years ago, with ox-teams, a dozen or two bags of wheat, threshed with a flail and winnowed with a wagon cover, and were camped for the night by the Calipoola River; for it took two days to reach the mill. Lyte got out his fiddle, keeping his gun, of course, close at hand. Pretty soon the oxen came down, came very close, so close that they almost put their cold, moist noses against the backs of our necks as we sat there on the ox-yokes or reclined in our blankets, around the crackling pine-log fire and listened to the wild, sweet strains that swept up and down and up till the very tree tops seemed to dance and quiver with delight.

Then suddenly father seemed to feel the presence of something or somebody strange, and I felt it, too. But the fiddler felt, heard, saw nothing but the divine, wild melody that made the very pine trees dance and quiver to their tips. Oh, for the pure, wild, sweet, plaintive music once more! the music of "Money Musk," "Zip Coon," "Ol' Dan Tucker" and all the other dear old airs that once made a thousand happy feet keep time on the puncheon floors from Hudson's bank to the Oregon. But they are no more, now. They have

11

passed away forever with the Indian, the pioneer, and the music-loving bear. It is strange how a man—I mean the natural man—will feel a presence long before he hears it or sees it. You can always feel the approach of a—but I forget. You are of another generation, a generation that only reads, takes thought at second hand only, if at all, and you would not understand; so let us get forward and not waste time in explaining the unexplainable to you.

Father got up, turned about, put me behind him, as an animal will its young, and peered back and down through the dense tangle of the deep river bank between two of the huge oxen which had crossed the plains with us; then he reached around and drew me to him with his left hand, pointing between the oxen sharp down the bank with his right forefinger.

A bear! two bears! and another coming; one already more than half way across on the great, mossy log that lay above the deep, sweeping waters of the Calipoola; and Lyte kept on, and the wild, sweet music leaped up and swept through the delighted and dancing boughs above. Then father reached back to the fire and thrust a long, burning bough deeper into the dying embers and the glittering sparks leaped and laughed and danced and swept out and up and up as if to companion with the stars. Then Lyte knew. He did not hear, he did not see, he only felt; but the fiddle forsook his fingers and his chin in a second, and his gun was to his face with the muzzle thrust down between the oxen. And then my father's gentle hand reached out, lay on that long, black, Kentucky rifle barrel, and it dropped down, slept once more at the fiddler's side, and again the melodies; and the very stars came down, believe me, to listen, for they never seemed so big and so close by before. The bears sat down on their haunches at last, and one of them kept opening his mouth and putting out his red tongue, as if he really wanted to taste the music. Every now and then one of them

12

would lift up a paw and gently tap the ground, as if to keep time with the music. And both my papa and Lyte said next day that those bears really wanted to dance.

And that is all there is to say about that, except that my father was the gentlest gentleman I ever knew and his influence must have been boundless; for who ever before heard of any hunter laying down his rifle with a family of fat black bears holding the little snow-white cross on their breasts almost within reach of its muzzle?

The moon came up by and by, and the chin of the weary fiddler sank lower and lower, till all was still. The oxen lay down and ruminated, with their noses nearly against us. Then the coal-black bears melted away before the milk-white moon, and we slept there, with the sweet breath of the cattle, like incense, upon us.

III

MY FIRST GRIZZLY

ONE OF FREMONT'S MEN, Mountain Joe, had taken a fancy to me down in Oregon, and finally, to put three volumes in three lines, I turned up as partner in his Soda Springs ranch on the Sacramento, where the famous Shasta water is now bottled, I believe. Then the Indians broke out, burned us up and we followed and fought them in Castle rocks, and I was shot down. Then my father came on to watch by my side, where I lay, under protection of soldiers, at the mouth of Shot Creek canyon.

As the manzanita berries began to turn the mountain sides red and the brown pine quills to sift down their perfumed carpets at our feet, I began to feel some strength and wanted to fight, but I had had enough of Indians. I wanted to fight grizzly bears this time. The fact is, they used to leave tracks in the pack trail every night, and right close about the camp, too, as big as the head of a barrel.

13

Now father was well up in woodcraft, no man better, but he never fired a gun. Never, in his seventy years of life among savages, did that gentle Quaker, schoolmaster, magistrate and Christian ever fire a gun. But he always allowed me to have my own way as a hunter, and now that I was getting well of my wound he was so glad and grateful that he willingly joined in with the soldiers to help me kill one of these huge bears that had made the big tracks.

Do you know why a beast, a bear of all beasts, is so very much afraid of fire? Well, in the first place, as said before, a bear is a gentleman, in dress as well as address, and so likes a decent coat. If a bear should get his coat singed he would hide away from sight of both man and beast for half a year. But back of his pride is the fact that a fat bear will burn like a candle; the fire will not stop with the destruction of his coat. And so, mean as it was, in the olden days, when bears were as common in California as cows are now, men used to take advantage of this fear and kindle pine-quill fires in and around his haunts in the head of canyons to drive him out and down and into ambush.

Read two or three chapters here between the lines—lots of plans, preparations, diagrams. I was to hide near camp and wait—to place the crescent of pine-quill fires and all that. Then at twilight they all went out and away on the mountain sides around the head of the canyon, and I hid behind a big rock near by the extinguished campfire, with my old muzzle-loading Kentucky rifle, lifting my eyes away up and around to the head of the Manzanita canyon looking for the fires. A light! One, two, three, ten! A sudden crescent of forked flames, and all the fight and impetuosity of a boy of only a dozen years was uppermost, and I wanted a bear!

All alone I waited; got hot, cold, thirsty, cross as a bear and so sick of sitting there that I was about to go to my blankets, for the flames had almost died out on the hills, leaving only a circle of little dots and dying embers, like a

He rose up, and rose up, and rose up!

fading diadem on the mighty lifted brow of the glorious Manzanita mountain. And now the new moon came, went softly and sweetly by, like a shy, sweet maiden, hiding down, down out of sight.

Crash! His head was thrown back, not over his shoulder, as you may read but never see, but down by his left foot, as he looked around and back up the brown mountain side. He had stumbled, or rather, he had stepped on himself, for a bear gets down hill sadly. If a bear ever gets after you, you had better go down hill and go down hill fast. It will make him mad, but that is not your affair. I never saw a bear go down hill in a good humor. What nature meant by making a bear so short in the arms I don't know. Indians say he was first a man and walked upright with a club on his shoulder, but sinned and fell. As evidence of this, they show that he can still stand up and fight with his fists when hard pressed.

This huge brute before me looked almost white in the tawny twilight as he stumbled down through the steep tangle of chaparral into the opening on the stony bar of the river.

He had evidently been terribly tangled up and disgusted while in the bush and jungle, and now, well out of it, with the foamy, rumbling, roaring Sacramento River only a few rods beyond him, into which he could plunge with his glossy coat, he seemed to want to turn about and shake his huge fists at the crescent of fire in the pine quills that had driven him down the mountain. He threw his enormous bulk back on his haunches and rose up, and rose up, and rose up! Oh, the majesty of this king of our continent, as he seemed to still keep rising! Then he turned slowly around on his great hinder feet to look back; he pushed his nose away out, then drew it back, twisted his short, thick neck, like that of a beer-drinking German, and then for a final observation he tiptoed up, threw his high head still higher in the air and wiggled it about and sniffed and sniffed and—bang!

17

I shot at him from ambush, with his back toward me, shot at his back! For shame! Henry Highton would not have done that; nor, indeed, would I or any other real sportsman do such a thing now; but I must plead the "Baby Act," and all the facts, and also my sincere penitence, and proceed.

The noble brute did not fall, but let himself down with dignity and came slowly forward. Hugely, ponderously, solemnly, he was coming. And right here, if I should set down what I thought about—where father was, the soldiers, anybody, everybody else, whether I had best just fall on my face and "play possum" and put in a little prayer or two on the side, like—well, I was going on to say that if I should write all that flashed and surged through my mind in the next three seconds, you would be very tired. I was certain I had not hit the bear at all. As a rule, you can always see the "fur fly," as hunters put it; only it is not fur, but dust, that flies.

But this bear was very fat and hot, and so there could have been no dust to fly. After shuffling a few steps forward and straight for the river, he suddenly surged up again, looked all about, just as before, then turned his face to the river and me, the tallest bear that ever tiptoed up and up and up in the Sierras. One, two, three steps—on came the bear! and my gun empty! Then he fell, all at once and all in a heap. No noise, no moaning or groaning at all, no clutching at the ground, as men have seen Indians and even white men do; as if they would hold the earth from passing away —nothing of that sort. He lay quite still, head down hill, on his left side, gave just one short, quick breath, and then, pulling up his great right paw, he pushed his nose and eyes under it, as if to shut out the light forever, or, maybe, to muffle up his face as when "great Caesar fell."

And that was all. I had killed a grizzly bear; nearly as big as the biggest ox.

18

IV

THESE TWIN BABIES were black. They were black as coal. Indeed, they were blacker than coal, for they glistened in their oily blackness. They were young baby bears; and so exactly alike that no one could, in any way, tell the one from the other. And they were orphans. They had been found at the foot of a small cedar tree on the banks of the Sacramento River, near the now famous Soda Springs, found by a tow-headed boy who was very fond of bears and hunting.

But at the time the twin babies were found Soda Springs was only a wild camp, or way station, on the one and only trail that wound through the woods and up and down mountains for hundreds of miles, connecting the gold fields of California with the pastoral settlements away to the north in Oregon. But a railroad has now taken the place of that tortuous old pack trail, and you can whisk through these wild and woody mountains, and away on down through Oregon and up through Washington, Montana, Dakota, Minnesota, Wisconsin and on to Chicago without even once getting out of your car, if you like. Yet such a persistent ride is not probable, for fish, pheasants, deer, elk, and bear still abound here in their ancient haunts, and the temptation to get out and fish or hunt is too great to be resisted.

This place where the baby bears were found was first owned by three men, or, rather, by two men and a boy. One of the men was known as Mountain Joe. He had once been a guide in the service of General Fremont, but he was now a drunken fellow and spent most of his time at the trading post, twenty miles down the river. He is now an old man, almost blind, and lives in Oregon City, on a pension received

19

as a soldier of the Mexican war. The other man's name was Sil Reese. He, also, is living and famously rich—as rich as he is stingy, and that is saying that he is very rich indeed.

The boy preferred the trees to the house, partly because it was more pleasant and partly because Sil Reese, who had a large nose and used it to talk with constantly, kept grumbling because the boy, who had been wounded in defending the ranch, was not able to work—wash the dishes, make fires and so on, and help in a general and particular way about the so-called "Soda Spring Hotel." This Sil Reese was certainly a mean man.

The baby bears were found asleep, and alone. How they came to be there, and, above all, how they came to be left long enough alone by their mother for a feeble boy to rush forward at sight of them, catch them up in his arms and escape with them, will always be a wonder. But this one thing is certain, you had about as well take up two rattlesnakes in your arms as two baby bears, and hope to get off unharmed, if the mother of the young bears is within a mile of you. This boy, however, had not yet learned caution, and he probably was not born with much fear in his make-up. And then he was so lonesome, and this man Reese was so cruel and so cross, with his big nose like a sounding foghorn, that the boy was glad to get even a bear to love and play with.

They, so far from being frightened or cross, began to root around under his arms and against his breast, like little pigs, for something to eat. Possibly their mother had been killed by hunters, for they were nearly famished. When he got them home, how they did eat! This also made Sil Reese mad. For, although the boy, wounded as he was, managed to shoot down a deer not too far from the house almost every day, and so kept the "hotel" in meat, still it made Reese miserable and envious to see the boy so happy with his sable and woolly little friends. Reese was simply mean!

Before a month the little black boys began to walk erect, carry stick muskets, wear paper caps, and march up and down before the door of the big log "hotel" like soldiers.

But the cutest trick they learned was that of waiting on the table. With little round caps and short white aprons, the little black boys would stand behind the long bench on which the guests sat at the pine board table and pretend to take orders with precision and solemnity.

Of course, it is to be confessed that they often dropped things, especially if the least bit hot; but remember we had only tin plates and tin or iron dishes of all sorts, so that little damage was done if a dish did happen to fall and rattle down on the earthen floor.

Men came from far and near and often lingered all day to see these cunning and intelligent creatures perform.

About this time Mountain Joe fought a duel with another mountaineer down at the trading post, and this duel, a bloodless and foolish affair, was all the talk. Why not have the little black fellows fight a duel also? They were surely civilized enough to fight now!

And so, with a very few days' training, they fought a duel exactly like the one in which poor, drunken old Mountain Joe was engaged; even to the detail of one of them suddenly dropping his stick gun and running away and falling headlong in a prospect hole.

When Joe came home and saw this duel and saw what a fool he had made of himself, he at first was furiously angry. But it made him sober, and he kept sober for half a year. Meantime Reese was mad as ever, more mad, in fact, than ever before. For he could not endure to see the boy have any friends of any kind. Above all, he did not want Mountain Joe to stay at home or keep sober. He wanted to handle all the money and answer no questions. A drunken man and a boy that he could bully suited him best. Ah, but this man Reese was a mean fellow, as has been said a time or two.

21

As winter came on the two blacks were fat as pigs and fully half-grown. Their appetites increased daily, and so did the anger and envy of Mr. Sil Reese.

"They'll eat us out o' house and hum," said the big, towering nose one day, as the snow began to descend and close up the pack trails. And then the stingy man proposed that the blacks should be made to hibernate, as others of their kind. There was a big, hollow log that had been sawed off in joints to make bee gums; and the stingy man insisted that they should be put in there with a tight head, and a pack of hay for a bed, and nailed up till spring to save provisions.

Soon there was an Indian outbreak. Some one from the ranch, or "hotel," must go with the company of volunteers that was forming down at the post for a winter campaign. Of course Reese would not go. He wanted Mountain Joe to go and get killed. But Joe was sober now and he wanted to stay and watch Reese.

And that is how it came about that the two black babies were tumbled headlong into a big, black bee gum, or short, hollow log, on a heap of hay, and nailed up for the winter. The boy had to go to the war.

It was late in the spring when the boy, having neglected to get himself killed, to the great disgust of Mr. Sil Reese, rode down and went straight up to the big, black bee gum in the back yard. He put his ear to a knothole. Not a sound. He tethered his mule, came back and tried to shake the short, hollow log. Not a sound or sign or movement of any kind. Then he kicked the big black gum with all his might. Nothing. Rushing to the woodpile, he caught up an ax and in a moment had the whole end of the big gum caved in, and, to his infinite delight, out rolled the twins!

But they were merely the ghosts of themselves. They had been kept in a month or more too long, and were now so weak and so lean that they could hardly stand on their feet.

22

"Kill 'em and put 'em out o' misery," said Reese, for run from him they really could not, and he came forward and kicked one of them flat down on its face as it was trying hard to stand on its four feet.

The boy had grown some; besides, he was just from the war and was now strong and well. He rushed up in front of Reese, and he must have looked unfriendly, for Sil Reese tried to smile, and then at the same time he turned hastily to go into the house. And when he got fairly turned around, the boy kicked him precisely where he had kicked the bear. And he kicked him hard, so hard that he pitched forward on his face just as the bear had done. He got up quickly, but he did not look back. He seemed to have something to do in the house.

In a month the babies, big babies now, were sleek and fat. It is amazing how these creatures will eat after a short nap of a few months, like that. And their cunning tricks, now! And their kindness to their master! Ah! their glossy black coats and their brilliant black eyes!

And now three men came. Two of these men were Italians from San Francisco. The third man was also from that city, but he had an amazing big nose and refused to eat bear meat. He thought it was pork.

They took tremendous interest in the big black twins, and stayed all night and till late next day, seeing them perform.

"Seventy-five dollars," said one big nose to the other big nose, back in a corner where they thought the boy did not hear.

"One hundred and fifty. You see, I'll have to give my friends fifty each. Yes, it's true I've took care of 'em all winter, but I ain't mean, and I'll only keep fifty of it."

The boy, bursting with indignation, ran to Mountain Joe with what he had heard. But poor Joe had been sober for a long time, and his eyes fairly danced in delight at having

23

fifty dollars in his own hand to spend down at the post. And so the two Italians muzzled the big, pretty pets and led them kindly down the trail toward the city, where they were to perform in the streets, the man with the big nose following after the twins on a big white mule.

And what became of the big black twin babies? They are still performing, seem content and happy, sometimes in a circus, sometimes in a garden, sometimes in the street. They are great favorites and have never done harm to anyone.

And what became of Sil Reese? Well, as said before, he still lives, is very rich and very miserable. He met the boy— the boy that was—on the street the other day and wanted to talk of old times. He told the boy he ought to write something about the old times and put him, Sil Reese, in it. He said, with that same old sounding nose and sickening smile, that he wanted the boy to be sure and put his, Sil Reese's name, in it so that he could show it to his friends. And the boy has done so.

The boy? You want to know what the boy is doing? Well, in about a second he will be signing his autograph to the bottom of this story about his twin babies.

V

IN SWIMMING WITH A BEAR

WHAT MADE THESE ugly rows of scars on my left hand? Well, it might have been buckshot; only it wasn't. Besides, buckshot would be scattered about, "sort of promiscuous like," as backwoodsmen say. But these ugly little holes are all in a row, or rather in two rows. Now a wolf might have made these holes with his fine white teeth, or a bear might have done it with his dingy and ugly teeth, long ago. I must here tell you that the teeth of a bear are not nearly so fine as the teeth of a wolf. And the teeth of a lion

24

are the ugliest of them all. They are often broken and bent; and they are always of a dim yellow color. It is from this yellow hue of the lion's teeth that we have the name of one of the most famous early flowers of May: dent de lion, tooth of the lion; dandelion.

I know of three men, all old men now, who have their left hands all covered with scars. One is due to the wolf; the others owe their scars to the red mouths of black bears.

You see, in the old days, out here in California, when the Sierras were full of bold young fellows hunting for gold, quite a number of them had hand-to-hand battles with bears. For when we came out here "the woods were full of 'em."

Of course, the first thing a man does when he finds himself face to face with a bear that won't run and he has no gun— and that is always the time when he finds a bear—why, he runs, himself; that is, if the bear will let him.

But it is generally a good deal like the old Crusader who "caught a Tartar" long ago, when on his way to capture Jerusalem, with Peter the Hermit.

"Come on!" cried Peter to the helmeted and knightly old Crusader, who sat his horse with lance in rest on a hill a little in the rear. "Come on!"

"I can't! I've caught a Tartar."

"Well, bring him along."

"He won't come."

"Well, then, come without him."

"He won't let me."

And so it often happened in the old days out here. When a man "caught" his bear and didn't have his gun he had to fight it out hand-to-hand. But fortunately, every man at all times had a knife in his belt. A knife never gets out of order, never "snaps," and a man in those days always had to have it with him to cut his food, cut brush, "crevice" for gold, and so on.

25

Oh! it is a grim picture to see a young fellow in his red shirt wheel about, when he can't run, thrust out his left hand, draw his knife with his right, and so, breast to breast, with the bear erect, strike and strike and strike to try to reach his heart before his left hand is eaten off to the elbow!

We have five kinds of bears in the Sierras. The "boxer," the "biter," the "hugger," are the most conspicuous. The other two are a sort of "all round" rough and tumble style of fighters.

The grizzly is the boxer. A game old beast he is, too, and would knock down all the John L. Sullivans you could put in the Sierras faster than you could set them up. He is a kingly old fellow and disdains familiarity. Whatever may be said to the contrary, he never "hugs" if he has room to box. In some desperate cases he has been known to bite, but ordinarily he obeys "the rules of the ring."

The cinnamon bear is a lazy brown brute, about one-half the size of the grizzly. He always insists on being very familiar, if not affectionate. This is the "hugger."

Next in order comes the big, sleek, black bear; easily tamed, too lazy to fight, unless forced to it. But when "cornered" he fights well, and, like a lion, bites to the bone.

After this comes the small and quarrelsome black bear with big ears, and a white spot on his breast. I have heard hunters say, but I don't quite believe it, that he sometimes points to this white spot on his breast as a sort of Free Mason's sign, as if to say, "Don't shoot." Next in order comes the smaller black bear with small ears. He is ubiquitous, as well as omniverous; gets into pigpens, knocks over your beehives, breaks open your milkhouse, eats more than two good-sized hogs ought to eat, and is off for the mountain top before you dream he is about. The first thing you see in the morning, however, will be some muddy tracks on the door steps. For he always comes and snuffles and shuffles and smells about the door in a good-natured sort of way, and leaves his card. The fifth member of the great bear family is not much bigger than an ordinary dog; but he is numerous, and he, too, is a nuisance.

Dog? Why not set the dog on him? Let me tell you. The California dog is a lazy, degenerate cur. He ought to be put with the extinct animals. He devotes his time and his talent to the flea. Not six months ago I saw a coon, on his way to my fishpond in the pleasant moonlight, walk within two feet of my dog's nose and not disturb his slumbers.

This last-named bear has a big head and small body; has a long, sharp nose and longer and sharper teeth than any of the others; he is a natural thief, has low instincts, carries his nose close to the ground, and, wherever possible, makes his road along on the mossy surface of fallen trees in humid forests. He eats fish—dead and decaying salmon—in such abundance that his flesh is not good in the salmon season.

It was with this last described specimen of the bear family that a precocious old boy who had hired out to some horse drovers went in swimming years and years ago. The two drovers had camped to recruit and feed their horses on the wild grass and clover that grew at the headwaters of the Sacramento River, close up under the foot of Mount Shasta. A pleasant spot it was, in the pleasant summer weather.

This warm afternoon the two men sauntered leisurely away up Soda Creek to where their horses were grazing belly deep in grass and clover. They were slow to return, and the boy, as all boys will, began to grow restless. He had fished, he had hunted, had diverted himself in a dozen ways, but now he wanted something new. He got it.

A little distance below camp could be seen, through the thick foliage that hung and swung and bobbed above the swift waters, a long, mossy log that lay far out and far above the cool, swift river.

Why not go down through the trees and go out on that log, take off his clothes, dangle his feet, dance on the moss,

27

do anything, everything that a boy wants to do? In two minutes the boy was out on the big, long, mossy log, kicking his boots off, and in two minutes more he was dancing up and down on the humid, cool moss, and as naked as the first man, when he was first made.

And it was very pleasant. The great, strong river splashed and dashed and boomed below; above him the long green branches hung dense and luxuriant and almost within reach. Far off and away through their shifting shingle he caught glimpses of the bluest of all blue skies. And a little to the left he saw gleaming in the sun and almost overhead the everlasting snows of Mount Shasta.

Putting his boots and his clothes all carefully in a heap, that nothing might roll off into the water, he walked, or rather danced on out to where the further end of the great fallen tree lay lodged on a huge boulder in the middle of the swift and surging river. His legs dangled down and he patted his plump thighs with great satisfaction. Then he leaned over and saw some gold and silver trout, then he flopped over and lay down on his breast to get a better look at them.

Then he thought he heard something behind him on the other end of the log! He pulled himself together quickly and stood erect, face about. There was a bear! It was one of those mean, sneaking, long-nosed, ant-eating little fellows, it is true, but it was a bear! And a bear is a bear to a boy, no matter about his size, age or character. The boy stood high up. The boy's bear stood up. And the boy's hair stood up!

The bear had evidently not seen the boy yet. But it had smelled his boots and clothes, and had got upon his dignity. But now, dropping down on all fours, with nose close to the mossy butt of the log, it slowly shuffled forward.

That boy was the stillest boy, all this time, that has ever been. Pretty soon the bear reached the clothes. He stopped,

28

He nosed them about as a hog might.

sat down, nosed them about as a hog might, and then slowly and lazily got up; but with a singular sort of economy of old clothes, for a bear, he did not push anything off into the river. What next?

Would he come any farther? Would he? Could he? Will he? The long sharp little nose was once more to the moss and sliding slowly and surely toward the poor boy's naked shins. Then the boy shivered and settled down, down, down on his haunches, with his little hands clasped till he was all of a heap.

He tried to pray, but somehow or another, all he could think of as he sat there crouched down with all his clothes off was: "Now I lay me down to sleep."

But all this could not last. The bear was almost on him in half a minute, although he did not lift his nose six inches till almost within reach of the boy's toes. Then the surprised bear suddenly stood up and began to look the boy in the face. As the terrified youth sprang up, he thrust out his left hand as a guard and struck the brute with all his might between the eyes with the other. But the left hand lodged in the two rows of sharp teeth and the boy and bear rolled into the river together.

But they were together only an instant. The bear, of course, could not breathe with his mouth open in the water, and so had to let go. Instinctively, or perhaps because his course lay in that direction, the bear struck out, swimming "dog fashion," for the farther shore. And as the boy certainly had no urgent business on that side of the river he did not follow, but kept very still, clinging to the moss on the big boulder till the bear had shaken the water from his coat and disappeared in the thicket.

Then the boy, pale and trembling from fright and the loss of blood, climbed up the broken end of the log, got his clothes, struggled into them as he ran, and so reached camp.

And he had not yelled! He tied up his hand in a piece of

old flour sack, all by himself, for the men had not yet got back; and he didn't whimper! And what became of the boy? you ask.

The boy grew up as all energetic boys do; for there seems to be a sort of special providence for such boys.

And where is he now?

Out in California, trapping bear in the winter and planting olive trees in their season.

And do I know him?

Yes, pretty well, almost as well as any old fellow can know himself.

VI

A FAT LITTLE EDITOR

MOUNT SINAI, Heart of the Sierras—this place is one mile east and a little less than one mile perpendicular from the hot, dusty and dismal little railroad town down on the rocky banks of the foaming and tumbling Sacramento River. Some of the old miners are down there still—still working on the desolate old rocky bars with rockers. They have been there, some of them, for more than thirty years. A few of them have little orchards, or vineyards, on the steep, overhanging hills, but there is no home life, no white women to speak of, as yet. The battered and gray old miners are poor, lonely and discouraged, but they are honest, stout-hearted still, and of a much higher type than those that hang about the towns. It is hot down on the river—too hot, almost, to tell the truth. Even here under Mount Shasta, in her sheets of eternal snow, the mercury is at par.

This Mount Sinai is not a town; it is a great spring of cold water that leaps from the high, rocky front of a mountain which we have located as a summer home in the Sierras— myself and a few other scribes of California.

This is the great bear land. One of our party, a simple-hearted and honest city editor, who was admitted into our little mountain colony because of his boundless good nature and native goodness, had never seen a bear before he came here. City editors do not, as a rule, ever know much about bears. This little city editor is bald-headed, bow-legged, plain to a degree. And maybe that is why he is so good. "Give me fat men," said Caesar.

But give me plain men for good men, any time. Pretty women are to be preferred; but pretty men? Bah! I must get on with the bear, however, and make a long story a short story. We found our fat, bent-legged editor from the city fairly broiling in the little railroad town, away down at the bottom of the hill in the yellow golden fields of the Sacramento; and he was so limp and so lazy that we had to lay hold of him and get him out of the heat and up into the heart of the Sierras by main force.

Only one hour of climbing and we got up to where the little mountain streams come tumbling out of snowbanks on every side. The Sacramento, away down below and almost under us, from here looks dwindled to a brawling brook; a foamy white thread twisting about the boulders as big as meeting houses, plunging forward, white with fear, as if glad to get away—as if there was a bear back there where it came from. We did not register. No, indeed. This place here on Square Creek, among the clouds, where the water bursts in a torrent from the living rock, we have named Mount Sinai. We own the whole place for one mile square—the tall pine trees, the lovely pine-wood houses; all, all. We proposed to hunt and fish, for food. But we had some bread, some bacon, lots of coffee and sugar. And so, whipping out our hooks and lines, we set off with the editor up a little mountain brook, and in less than an hour were far up among the fields of eternal snow, and finely loaded with trout.

33

What a bed of pine quills! What long and delicious cones for a campfire! Some of those sugar-pine cones are as long as your arm. One of them alone will make a lofty pyramid of flame and illuminate the scene for half a mile about. I threw myself on my back and kicked up my heels. I kicked care square in the face. Oh, what freedom! How we would rest after dinner here! Of course we could not all rest or sleep at the same time. One of us would have to keep a pine cone burning all the time. Bears are not very numerous out here; but the Californian lion is both numerous and large here. The wildcat, too, is no friend to the tourist. But we were not tourists. The land was and is ours. We would and all could defend our own.

The sun was going down. Glorious! The shades of night were coming up out of the gorges below and audaciously pursuing the dying sun. Not a sound. Not a sign of man or of beast. We were scattered all up and down the hill.

Crash! Something came tearing down the creek through the brush! The fat and simple-hearted editor, who had been dressing the homeopathic dose of trout, which inexperience had marked as his own, sprang up from the bank of the tumbling little stream above us and stood at his full height. His stout little knees for the first time smote together. I was a good way below him on the steep hillside. A brother editor was slicing bacon on a piece of reversed pine bark close by.

"Fall down," I cried, "fall flat down on your face."

It was a small she bear, and she was very thin and very hungry, with cubs at her heels, and she wanted that fat little city editor's flesh. I know it would take volumes to convince you that I really meant for the bear to pass by him and come after me and my friend with both fish and bacon, and so, with half a line, I assert this truth and pass on. Nor was I in any peril in appropriating the little brown bear to myself. Any man who knows what he is about is as safe with a bear on a steep hillside as is the best bullfighter in any arena. No bear can keep his footing on a steep hillside, much less fight. And whenever an Indian is in peril he always takes down hill till he comes to a steep plane, and then lets the bear almost overtake him, when he suddenly steps aside and either knifes the bear to the heart or lets the open-mouthed beast go on down the hill, heels over head.

The fat editor turned his face toward me, and it was pale. "What! Lie down and be eaten up while you lie there and kick up your heels and enjoy yourself? Never. We will die together!" he shouted.

He started for me as fast as his short legs would allow. The bear struck at him with her long, rattling claws. He landed far below me, and when he got up he hardly knew where he was or what he was. His clothes were in shreds, the back and bottom parts of them. The bear caught at his trout and was gone in an instant back with her two little cubs, and a moment later the little family had dined and was away, over the hill. She was a cinnamon bear, not much bigger than a big, yellow dog, and almost as lean and mean and hungry as any wolf could possibly be. We helped our inexperienced little friend slowly down to camp, forgetting all about the bacon and the fish till we came to the little board house, where we had coffee. Of course the editor could not go to the table now. He leaned, or rather sat, against a pine, drank copious cups of coffee and watched the stars, while I heaped up great piles of leaves and built a big fire, and so night rolled by in all her starry splendor as the men slept soundly all about beneath the lordly pines. But alas for the fat little editor; he did not like the scenery, and he would not stay. We saw him to the station on his way back to his little sanctum. He said he was satisfied. He had seen the "bar." His last words were, as he pulled himself close together in a modest corner in the car and smiled feebly: "Say, boys, you won't let it get in the papers, will you?"

35

VII

AWAY BACK in the "fifties" bears were as numerous on the banks of the Willamette River, in Oregon, as are hogs in the hickory woods of Kentucky in nut time, and that is saying that bears were mighty plenty in Oregon about forty years ago.

You see, after the missionaries established their great cattle ranches in Oregon and gathered the Indians from the wilderness and set them to work and fed them on beef and bread, the bears had it all their own way, till they literally overran the land. And this gave a great chance for sport to the sons of missionaries and the sons of new settlers.

And it was not perilous sport, either, for the grizzly was rarely encountered here. His home was further to the south. Neither was the large and clumsy cinnamon bear abundant on the banks of the beautiful Willamette in those dear old days, when you might ride from sun to sun, belly deep in wild flowers, and never see a house. But the small black bear, as indicated before, was on deck in great force, at all times and in nearly all places.

It was the custom in those days for boys to take this bear with the lasso, usually on horseback.

We would ride along close to the dense woods that grew by the river bank, and, getting between him and his base of retreat, would, as soon as we sighted a bear feeding out in the open plain, swing our lassos and charge him with whoop and yell. His habit of rearing up and standing erect and looking about to see what was the matter made him an easy prey to the lasso. And then the fun of taking him home through the long, strong grass!

As a rule, he did not show fight when once in the toils of

the lasso; but in a few hours, making the best of the situation like a little philosopher, he would lead along like a dog.

There were, of course, exceptions to this exemplary conduct. On one occasion particularly, Ed Parish, the son of a celebrated missionary, came near losing his life by counting too confidently on the docility of a bear which he had taken with a lasso and was leading home.

His bear suddenly stopped, stood up and began to haul in the rope, hand over hand, just like a sailor. And as the other end of the rope was fastened tightly to the big Spanish pommel of the saddle, why of course the distance between the bear and the horse soon grew perilously short, and Ed Parish slid from his horse's back and took to the brush, leaving horse and bear to fight it out as best they could.

When he came back, with some boys to help him, the horse was dead and the bear was gone, having cut the rope with his teeth.

After having lost his horse in this way, poor little Ed Parish had to do his hunting on foot, and, as my people were immigrants and very poor, why we, that is my brother and I, were on foot also. This kept us three boys together a great deal, and many a peculiar adventure we had in those dear days "when all the world was young."

Ed Parish was nearly always the hero of our achievements, for he was a bold, enterprising fellow, who feared nothing at all. In fact, he finally lost his life from his very great love of adventure. But this is too sad to tell now, and we must be content with the story about how he treed a bear for the present.

We three boys had gone bear hunting up a wooded canyon near his father's ranch late one warm summer afternoon. Ed had a gun, but, as I said before, my people were very poor, so neither brother nor I as yet had any other arms or implements than the inseparable lasso.

Ed, who was always the captain in such cases, chose the

center of the dense, deep canyon for himself, and, putting
my brother on the hillside to his right and myself on the
hillside to his left, ordered a simultaneous "Forward
march." After a time we heard him shoot. Then we heard
him shout. Then there was a long silence.

Then suddenly, high and wild, his voice rang out through
the tree tops down in the deep canyon.

"Come down! Come quick! I've treed a bear! Come and
help me catch him; come quick! Oh, Moses! come quick,
and—and—and catch him!"

My brother came tearing down the steep hill on his side
of the canyon as I descended from my side. We got down
about the same time, but the trees in their dense foliage,
together with the compact underbrush, concealed everything. We could see neither bear nor boy.

This Oregon is a damp country, warm and wet; nearly
always moist and humid, and so the trees are covered with
moss. Long, gray, sweeping moss swings from the broad,
drooping boughs of fir and pine and cedar and nearly every
bit of sunlight is shut out in these canyons from one year's
end to the other. And it rains here nearly half of the year;
and then these densely wooded canyons are as dark as
caverns. I know of nothing so grandly gloomy as these dense
Oregon woods in this long rainy season.

I laid my ear to the ground after I got a glimpse of my
brother on the other side of the canyon, but could hear
nothing at all but the beating of my heart.

Suddenly there was a wild yell away up in the dense
boughs of a big mossy maple tree that leaned over toward
my side of the canyon. I looked and looked with eagerness,
but could see nothing whatever.

Then again came the yell from the top of the big leaning
maple. Then there was a moment of silence, and then the
cry: "Oh, Moses! Why don't you come, I say, and help me
catch him?"

He had treed the bear, sure enough!

By this time I could see the leaves rustling. And I could see the boy rustling, too. And just behind him was a bear. He had treed the bear, sure enough!

My eyes gradually grew accustomed to the gloom and density, and I now saw the red mouth of the bear amid the green foliage high overhead. The bear had already pulled off one of Ed's boots and was about making a bootjack of his big red mouth for the other.

"Why don't you come on, I say, and help me catch him?"

He kicked at the bear, and at the same time hitched himself a little further along up the leaning trunk, and in doing so kicked his remaining boot into the bear's mouth.

"Oh, Moses, Moses! Why don't you come? I've got a bear, I tell you."

"Where is it, Ed?" shouted my brother on the other side.

But Ed did not tell him, for he had not yet got his foot from the bear's mouth, and was now too busy to do anything but yell and cry "Oh, Moses!"

Then my brother and I shouted out to Ed at the same time. This gave him great courage. He said something like "Confound you!" to the bear, and getting his foot loose without losing the boot he kicked the bear right on the nose. This brought things to a standstill. Ed hitched along a little higher up, and as the leaning trunk of the tree was already bending under his own and the bear's weight, the infuriated brute did not seem disposed to go further. Besides, as he had been mortally wounded, he was probably growing too weak to do much now.

My brother got to the bottom of the canyon and brought Ed's gun to where I stood. But, as we had no powder or bullets, and as Ed could not get them to us, even if he would have been willing to risk our shooting at the bear, it was hard to decide what to do. It was already dusk and we could not stay there all night.

"Boys," shouted Ed, at last, as he steadied himself in the

41

forks of a leaning and overhanging bough, "I'm going to come down on my laz rope. There, take that end of it, tie your laz ropes to it and scramble up the hill."

We obeyed him to the letter, and as we did so, he fastened his lasso firmly to the leaning bough and descended like a spider to where we had stood a moment before. We all scrambled up out of the canyon together and as quickly as possible. When we went back next day to get our ropes we found the bear dead near the root of the old mossy maple. The skin was a splendid one, and Ed insisted that my brother and I should have it, and we gladly accepted it.

My brother, who was older and wiser than I, said that he made us take the skin so that we would not be disposed to tell how he had "treed a bear." But I trust not, for he was a very generous-hearted fellow. Anyhow, we never told the story while he lived.

VIII

BILL CROSS AND HIS PET BEAR

WHEN MY FATHER settled down at the foot of the Oregon Sierras with his little family, long, long years ago, it was about forty miles from our place to the nearest civilized settlement.

People were very scarce in those days, and bears, as said before, were very plenty. We also had wolves, wildcats, wild cattle, wild hogs, and a good many long-tailed and big-headed yellow Californian lions.

The wild cattle, brought there from Spanish Mexico, next to the bear, were most to be feared. They had long, sharp horns and keen, sharp hoofs. Nature had gradually helped them out in these weapons of defense. They had grown to be slim and trim in body, and were as supple and swift as deer. They were the deadly enemies of all wild beasts; because all wild beasts devoured their young.

42

When fat and saucy, in warm summer weather, these cattle would hover along the foothills in bands, hiding in the hollows, and would begin to bellow whenever they saw a bear or a wolf, or even a man or boy, if on foot, crossing the wide valley of grass and blue camas blossoms. Then there would be music!

They would start up, with heads and tails in the air, and, broadening out, left and right, they would draw a long bent line, completely shutting off their victim from all approach to the foothills. If the unfortunate victim were a man or boy on foot, he generally made escape up one of the small ash trees that dotted the valley in groves here and there, and the cattle would then soon give up the chase. But if it were a wolf or any other wild beast that could not get up a tree, the case was different.

Far away, on the other side of the valley, where dense woods lined the banks of the winding Willamette River, the wild, bellowing herd would be answered. Out from the edge of the woods would stream, right and left, two long, corresponding, surging lines, bellowing and plunging forward now and then, their heads to the ground, their tails always in the air and their eyes aflame, as if they would set fire to the long gray grass. With the precision and discipline of a well-ordered army, they would close in upon the wild beast, too terrified now to either fight or fly, and, leaping upon him, one after another, with their long, sharp hoofs, he would, in a little time, be crushed into an unrecognizable mass. Not a bone would be left unbroken. It is a mistake to suppose that they ever used their long, sharp horns in attack. These were used only in defense, the same as elk or deer, falling on the knees and receiving the enemy on their horns.

Bill Cross was a "tenderfoot" at the time of which I write, and a sailor, at that. Now, the old pilgrims who had dared the plains in those days of '49, when cowards did not venture and the weak died on the way, had not the greatest respect for the courage or endurance of those who had reached Oregon by ship. But here was this man, a sailor by trade, settling down in the interior of Oregon, and, strangely enough, pretending to know more about everything in general and bears in particular than my father or his boys!

He had taken up a piece of land down in the pretty Camas Valley where the grass grew long and strong and waved in the wind, mobile and beautiful as the mobile sea.

The good-natured and self-complacent old sailor liked to watch the waving grass. It reminded him of the sea, I reckon. He would sometimes sit on our little porch as the sun went down and tell us boys strange, wild sea stories. He had traveled far and seen much, as much as any man can see on water, and maybe was not a very big liar, for a sailor, after all. We liked his tales. He would not work, and so he paid his way with stories of the sea. The only thing about him that we did not like, outside of his chronic idleness, was his exalted opinion of himself and his unconcealed contempt for everybody's opinion but his own.

"Bill," said my father one day, "those black Spanish cattle will get after that red sash and sailor jacket of yours some day when you go down in the valley to your claim, and they won't leave a grease spot. Better go horseback, or at least take a gun, when you go down next time."

"Pshaw! Squire. I wish I had as many dollars as I ain't afeard of all the black Spanish cattle in Oregon. Why, if they're so blasted dangerous, how did your missionaries ever manage to drive them up here from Mexico, anyhow?"

Still, for all that, the very next time that he saw the old sailor setting out at his snail pace for his ranch below, slow and indolent as if on the deck of a ship, my father insisted that he should go on horseback, or at least take a gun.

"Pooh, pooh! I wouldn't be bothered with a horse or a gun. Say, I'm goin' to bring your boys a pet bear some day."

44

And so, cocking his little hat down over his right eye and thrusting his big hands into his deep pockets almost to the elbows, he slowly and lazily whistled himself down the gradual slope of the foothills, waist deep in the waving grass and delicious wild flowers, and soon was lost to sight in the great waving sea.

Two things may be here written down. He wouldn't ride a horse because he couldn't, and for the same reason he wouldn't use a gun. Again let it be written down, also, that the reason he was going away that warm autumn afternoon was that there was some work to do. These facts were clear to my kind and indulgent father; but of course we boys never thought of it, and laid our little shoulders to the hard work of helping father lift up the long, heavy poles that were to complete the corral around our pioneer log cabin, and we really hoped and half believed that he might bring home a little pet bear.

This stout log corral had become an absolute necessity. It was high and strong, and made of poles or small logs stood on end in a trench, after the fashion of a primitive fort or stout stockade. There was but one opening, and that was a very narrow one in front of the cabin door. Here it was proposed to put up a gate. We also had talked about portholes in the corners of the corral, but neither gate nor portholes were yet made. In fact, as said before, the serene and indolent man of the sea always slowly walked away down through the grass toward his untracked claim whenever there was anything said about portholes, posts or gates.

Father and we three little boys had only just got the last post set and solidly "tamped" in the ground as the sun was going down.

Suddenly we heard a yell; then a yelling, then a bellowing. The yelling was heard in the high grass in the Camas Valley below, and the bellowing of cattle came from the woody river banks far beyond.

45

Then up on the brown hills of the Oregon Sierras above us came the wild answer of the wild black cattle of the hills, and a moment later, right and left, the long black lines began to widen out; then down they came, like a whirlwind, toward the black and surging line in the grass below. We were now almost in the center of what would, in a little time, be a complete circle and cyclone of furious Spanish cattle.

And now, here is something curious to relate. Our own cows, poor, weary, immigrant cows of only a year before, tossed their tails in the air, pawed the ground, bellowed and fairly went wild in the splendid excitement and tumult. One touch of nature made the whole cow world kin!

Father clambered up on a "buck-horse" and looked out over the stockade; and then he shouted and shook his hat and laughed as I had never heard him laugh before. For there, breathless, coatless, hatless, came William Cross, Esq., two small wolves and a very small black bear! They were all making good time, anywhere, anyway, to escape the frantic cattle. Father used to say afterwards, when telling about this little incident, that "it was nip and tuck between the four, and hard to say which was ahead." The cattle had made quite a "round-up."

They all four straggled in at the narrow little gate at about the same time, the great big, lazy sailor in a hurry, for the first time in his life.

But think of the coolness of the man, as he turned to us children with his first gasp of breath, and said, "Bo— bo— boys, I've bro— bro— brought you a little bear!"

The wolves were the little chicken thieves known as coyotes, quite harmless, as a rule, so far as man is concerned, but the cattle hated them and they were terrified nearly to death.

The cattle stopped a few rods from the stockade. We let the coyotes go, but we kept the little bear and named him Bill Cross. Yet he was never a bit cross, despite his name.

IX

NOT LONG AGO, about the time a party of Americans were setting out for India to hunt the tiger, a young banker from New York came to California to hunt what he rightly considered the nobler beast.

He chartered a small steamer in San Francisco Bay and taking with him a party of friends, as well as a great-grandson of Daniel Boone, a famous hunter, for a guide, he sailed up the coast to the redwood wilderness of Humboldt. Here he camped on the bank of a small stream in a madrona thicket and began to hunt for his bear. He found his bear, an old female with young cubs. As Boone was naturally in advance when the beast was suddenly stumbled upon, he had to do the fighting, and this gave the banker from the States a chance to scramble up a small madrona. Of course he dropped his gun. They always do drop their guns, by some singularly sad combination of accidents, when they start up a tree with two rows of big teeth in the rear, and it is hardly fair to expect the young bear-hunter from New York to prove an exception. Poor Boone was severely maltreated by the savage old mother grizzly in defense of her young. There was a crashing of brush and a crushing of bones, and then all was still.

Suddenly the bear seemed to remember that there was a second party who had been in earnest search for a bear, and looking back down the trail and up in the boughs of a small tree, she saw a pair of boots. She left poor Boone senseless on the ground and went for those boots. Coming forward, she reared up under the tree and began to claw for the capitalist. He told me that she seemed to him, as she stood there, to be about fifty feet high. Then she laid hold of the tree.

47

Fortunately this madrona tree is of a hard and unyielding nature, and with all her strength she could neither break nor bend it. But she kept thrusting up her long nose and longer claws, laying hold first of his boots, which she pulled off, one after the other, with her teeth, then with her claws she took hold of one garment and then another till the man of money had hardly a shred, and his legs were streaming with blood. Fearing that he should faint from loss of blood, he lashed himself to the small trunk of the tree by his belt and then began to scream with all his might for his friends.

When the bear became weary of clawing up at the dangling legs she went back and began to turn poor Boone over to see if he showed any signs of life. Then she came back and again clawed a while at the screaming man up the madrona tree. It was great fun for the bear!

To cut a thrilling story short, the party in camp on the other side of the creek finally came in hail, when the old bear gathered up her babies and made safe exit up a gulch. Boone, now in Arizona, was so badly crushed and bitten that his life was long despaired of, but he finally got well. The bear, he informed me, showed no disposition to eat him while turning him over and tapping him with her foot and thrusting her nose into his bleeding face to see if he still breathed.

Story after story of this character could be told to prove that the grizzly at home is not entirely brutal and savage; but rather a good-natured lover of his family and fond of his sly joke.

X

THE OLD KING

GENERAL FREMONT found this powerful brute to be a gregarious and confiding creature, fond of his family and not given to disturbing those who did not disturb him. In his report to the government—1847—he tells of finding

Several huge grizzlies were gathering and eating the acorns.

a large family of grizzly bears gathering acorns very much as the native Indians gathered them, and this not far from a small Mexican town. He says that riding at the head of his troops he saw, on reaching the brow of a little grassy hill set with oaks, a great commotion in the boughs of one of the largest trees, and, halting to cautiously reconnoiter, he noticed that there were grouped about the base of the tree and under its wide boughs, several huge grizzlies, employed in gathering and eating the acorns which the baby grizzlies threw down from the thick branches overhead. More than this, he reports that the baby bears, on seeing him, became frightened, and attempted to descend to the ground and run away, but the older bears, which had not yet discovered the explorers, beat the young ones and drove them back up the tree, and compelled them to go on with their work, as if they had been children.

In the early '50s, I, myself, saw the grizzlies feeding together in numbers under the trees, far up the Sacramento Valley, as tranquilly as a flock of sheep. A serene, dignified and very decent old beast was the full-grown grizzly as Fremont and others found him here at home. This king of the continent, who is quietly abdicating his throne, has never been understood. The grizzly was not only every inch a king, but he had, in his undisputed dominion, a pretty fair sense of justice. He was never a roaring lion. He was never a man-eater. He is indebted for his character for ferocity almost entirely to tradition, but, in some degree, to the female bear when seeking to protect her young.

Of course, the grizzlies are good fighters, when forced to it; but as for lying in wait for anyone, like the lion, or creeping, catlike, as the tiger does, into camp to carry off someone for supper, such a thing was never heard of in connection with the grizzly.

The grizzly went out as the American rifle came in. I do not think he retreated. He was a lover of home and family,

51

and so fell where he was born. For he is still found here and there, all up and down the land, as the Indian is still found, but he is no longer the majestic and serene king of the world. His whole life has been disturbed, broken up; and his temper ruined. He is a cattle thief now, and even a sheep thief. In old age, he keeps close to his canyon by day, deep in the impenetrable chaparral, and at night shuffles down hill to some hogpen, perfectly careless of dogs or shots, and, tearing out a whole side of the pen, feeds his fill on the inmates.

One of the interior counties kept a standing reward for the capture of an old grizzly of this character for several years. But he defied everything and he escaped everything but old age. Some hunters finally crept in to where the old king lay, nearly blind and dying of old age, and dispatched him with a volley from several Winchester rifles. It was found that he was almost toothless, his paws had been terribly mutilated by numerous steel traps, and it is said that his kingly old carcass had received nearly lead enough to sink a small ship.

There were no means of ascertaining his exact weight, but it was claimed that skin, bone and bullets, as he was found, he would have weighed well nigh a ton.

XI

THE BEAR WITH SPECTACLES

AND NOW LET US GO down to near the mouth of the Father of Waters, to "Barra Tarra Land" or Barren Land, as it was called of old by Cervantes, in the kingdom of Sancho Panza. Barra Tarra, so called, is the very richest part of this globe. It must have been rich always, rich as the delta of the Nile; but now, with the fertility of more than a dozen States dumped along there annually, it is rich as cream is rich.

The fish, fowl, oysters of Barra Tarra—ah, the oysters! No oysters in the world like these for flavor, size and sweetness. They are so enormous in size that—but let me illustrate their size by an anecdote of the war.

A Yankee captain, hungry and worn out hewing his way with his sword from Chicago to the sea, as General Logan had put it, sat down in a French restaurant in New Orleans, and while waiting for a plate of the famous Barra Tarra raw oysters, saw that a French creole sitting at the same little side table was turning over and over with his fork a solitary and most tempting oyster of enormous size, and eyeing it ruefully.

"Why don't you eat him?"

"By gar! I find him too big for me. You like?"

"Certainly. Not too big for me. See this!" and snatching the fork from the Frenchman the oyster was gone at a gulp.

The little Frenchman shrugged his shoulders, looked at the gallant officer a moment and then said in a fit of enthusiastic admiration:

"By gar, Monsieur Capitaine, you are one mighty brave man! I did try him t'ree times zat way, but he no stay."

The captain threw up his arms and—his oyster!—so runs the story.

The soil along the river bank is so rich that weeds, woods, vines, trench close and hard on the heels of the plowman. A plantation will almost perish from the earth, as it were, by a few years of abandonment. And so it is that you see miles and miles on either side—parishes on top of parishes, in fact —fast returning to barbarism, dragging the blacks by thousands down to below the level of brutes with them, as you descend from New Orleans toward the mouth of the mighty river, nearly one hundred miles from the beautiful "Crescent City." And, ah, the superstition of these poor blacks!

You see hundreds of little white houses, old "quarters," and all tenantless now, save one or two on each plantation.

53

Cheap sugar and high wages, as compared with old times of slavery—but then the enormous cost of keeping up the levees, and above all, the continued peril to life and property, with a mile of swift, muddy water sweeping seaward high above your head—these things are making a desert of the richest lands on earth. We are gaining ground in the West, but we are losing ground in the South, the great, silent South.

Of course, the world, we, civilization, will turn back to this wondrous region some day, when we have settled the West; for the mouth of the mightiest river on the globe is a fact; it is the mouth by which this young nation was trained in its younger days, and we cannot ignore it in the end, however willing we may be to do so now.

Strange how wild beasts and all sorts of queer creatures are overrunning the region down there, too, growing like weeds, increasing as man decreases. I found a sort of marsh bear here. He looks like the sloth bear (Ursus Labiatus) of the Ganges, India, as you see him in the Zoo of London, only he is not a sloth, by any means. The negroes are superstitiously afraid of him, and their dogs, very numerous, and good coon dogs, too, will not touch him. His feet are large and flat, to accommodate him in getting over the soft ground, while his shaggy and misshapen body is very thin and light. His color is as unlovely as his shape—a sort of faded, dirty brown or pale blue, with a rim of dirty white about the eyes that makes him look as if he wore spectacles when he stops and looks at you.

As he is not fit to eat because he lives on fish and oysters, sportsmen will not fire at him; and as the poor, superstitious, voodoo-worshipping negroes, and their dogs, too, run away as soon as he is seen, he has quite a habit of stopping and looking at you through his queer spectacles as long as you are in sight. He looks to be a sort of secondhand bear, his shaggy, faded, dirty coat of hair looking as if he had been stuffed, like an old sofa, with the stuffing coming out—a very secondhand appearance, to be sure.

Now, as I have always had a fondness for skins—having slept on them and under them all my life, making both bed and carpet of them—I very much wanted a skin of this queer marsh bear which the poor negroes both adore and dread as a sort of devil. But, as no one liked him well enough to kill him, I must do it myself; and with this object, along with my duty to describe the drowning plantations, I left New Orleans with Colonel Bloom, two good guns, and something to eat and to drink, and swept down the great river to the landing in the outer edge of the timber belt.

And how strange this landing! As a rule you have to climb up to the shore from a ship. Here, after setting foot on the levee, we walked down, down, down to reach the level land —a vast field of fevers.

I had a letter of introduction to the "preacher." He was a marvel of rags, preached every day and night, up and down the river, and received twenty-five cents a day from the few impoverished white planters, too poor to get away, for his influence for good among the voodoo blacks. Not that they could afford to care for the negroes, those few discouraged and fever-stricken planters on their plantations of weeds and water, but they must, now and then, have these indolent and retrograding blacks to plant or cut down their cane, or sow and gather their drowning patches of rice, and the preacher could preach them into working a little, when right hungry. The ragged black took my letter and pretended to read it. Poor fellow, he could not read, but pride, or rather vanity, made him act a lie. Seeing the fact, I contrived to tell him that it was from a colored clergyman, and that I had come to get him and his dogs to help me kill a bear. The blacks now turned white; or at least white around the lips. The preacher shuddered and shrugged his shoulders and finally groaned in his grief.

Let us omit the mosquitoes, the miserable babies, nude as nature, and surely very hungry in this beauteous place of fertility. They hung about my door, a "quarters" cabin with grass knee high through the cracks in the floor, like flies, till they got all my little store of supplies, save a big flask of "provisions" which General Beauregard had given me for Colonel Bloom, as a preventive against the deadly fever. No, it was not whiskey, not all whiskey, at least, for it was bitter as gall with quinine. I had to help the Colonel sample it at first, but I only helped him sample it once. It tasted so vile that it seemed to me I should, as between the two, prefer fever.

And such a moon! The ragged minister stood whooping up his numerous dogs and gathering his sullen clan of blacks to get that bear and that promised five dollars.

Away from up toward New Orleans, winding, sweeping, surging, flashing like a mighty sword of silver, the Father of Waters came through the air, high above our heads and level with the topmost limit of his artificial banks. The blacks were silent, ugly, sullen, and so the preacher asked for and received the five silver dollars in advance. This made me suspicious, and, out of humor, I went into my cabin and took Colonel Bloom into a corner and told him what had been done. He did not say one word but took a long drink of preventive against the fever, as General Beauregard had advised and provided.

Then we set out for the woods, through weeds that reached to our shoulders, the negroes in a string, slow, silent, sullen and ugly, the brave bear dogs only a little behind the negroes. The preacher kept muttering a monotonous prayer.

But that moon and that mighty sword of silver in the air, the silence, the large solemnity, the queer line of black heads barely visible above the sea of weeds! I was not right certain that I had lost any bear as we came to the edge of the moss-swept cypress woods, for here the negroes all suddenly

56

huddled up and muttered and prayed with one voice. Aye, how they prayed in their piteous monotone! How sad it all was!

The dogs had sat down a few rods back, a line of black dots along the path through the tall weeds, and did not seem to care for anything at all. I had to lay my hand on the preacher's shoulder and ask him to please get on; then they all started on together, and oh, the moon, through the swaying cypress moss, the mighty river above!

It was with great effort that I got them to cross a foot-log that lay across a lagoon only a little way in the moss-hung woods, the brave dogs all the time only a short distance behind us still. It was a hot night and the mosquitoes were terrible in the woods, but I doubt if they bite the blacks as they did me. Surely not, else they would not be even as nearly alive as they are.

Having got them across the lagoon, I gave them each twenty-five cents more, and this made them want to go home. The dogs had all sat down in a queer row on the foot-log. Such languor, such laziness, such idiotic helplessness I never saw before, even on the Nile. The blacks, as well as the dogs, seemed to be afraid to move now. The preacher again began to mumble a prayer, and the whole pack with him; and then they prayed again, this time not so loudly. And although there was melody of a sort in their united voices, I am certain they used no words, at least no words of any real language.

Suddenly the dogs got up and came across and hid among the men, and the men huddled up close; for right there on the other end of the log, with his broad right foot resting on it, was the shaggy little beast we were hunting for. We had found our bear, or rather, he had found us, and it was clear that he meant to come over and interview us at once.

The preacher crouched behind me as I cocked and raised my gun, the blacks hid behind the preacher, and I think, though I had not time to see certainly, that the dogs hid behind the blacks. I fired at the dim white spot on the bear's breast and sent shot after shot into his tattered coat, for he was not ten lengths of an old Kentucky ramrod distant, and he fell dead where he stood, and I went over and dragged him safely up on the higher bank.

Then the wild blacks danced and sang and sang and danced, till one of them slipped and fell into the lagoon. They fished him out and all returned to where I was, with the dead bear, dogs and all in great good spirits. Tying the bear's feet together with a withe they strung him on a pole and we all went back home, the blacks singing some barbaric half French song at the tops of their melodious voices.

But Colonel Bloom was afraid that the one who had fallen in the river might take the fever, and so as soon as we got safe back he drank what was left in the bottle General Beauregard had sent him and he went to sleep; while the superstitious blacks huddled together under the great levee and skinned the bear in the silver moonlight, below the mighty river. I gave them each a silver dollar—very bright was the brand new silver from the mint of New Orleans, but not nearly so bright as the moon away down there by the glowing rim of the Mexican seas where the spectacled bear abides in Barra Tarra, Kingdom of Sancho Panza.

XII

THE BEAR-SLAYER OF SAN DIEGO

LET US NOW LEAVE the great grizzly and the little marsh bear in spectacles behind us and tell about a boy, a bear-slayer; not about a bear, mind you. For the little fish-eating black bear which he killed and by which he got his name is hardly worth telling about. This bear lives in the brush along the sea-bank on the Mexican and Southern California coast and has huge feet but almost no hair. I

58

don't know any name for him, but think he resembles the "sun bear" (Ursus Titanus) more than any other. His habit of rolling himself up in a ball and rolling down hill after you is like that of the porcus or pig bear.

You may not know that a bear, any kind of a bear, finds it hard work running down hill, because of his short arms, so when a man who knows anything about bears is pursued, or thinks he is pursued, he always tries, if he knows himself, to run down hill. A man can escape almost any bear by running down hill, except this little fellow along the foothills by the Mexican seas. You see, he has good bear sense, like the rest of the bear family, and gets along without regard to legs of any sort, sometimes.

This boy that I am going to tell about was going to school on the Mexican side of the line between the two republics, near San Diego, California, when a she bear which had lost her cub caught sight of the boys at play down at the bottom of a high, steep hill, and she rolled for them, rolled right among the little, half-naked fellows, and knocked numbers of them down. But before she could get the dust out of her eyes and get up, this boy jumped on her and killed her with his knife.

The governor remembered the boy for his pluck and presence of mind and he was quite a hero and was always called "The Bear-Slayer" after that.

Some rich ladies from Boston, hearing about his brave act, put their heads together and then put their hands in their pockets and sent him to a higher school, where the following incident took place.

I ought to mention that this little Mexican bear, though he has but little hair on his body, has a great deal on his feet, making him look as if he wore pantalets, little short pantalets badly frayed out at the bottoms.

San Diego is one of the great new cities of Southern California. It lies within only a few minutes' ride of Mexico.

There is a pretty little Mexican town on the line between Mexico and California—Tia Juana—pronounced Te Wanna. Translated, the name means "Aunt Jane." In the center of one of the streets stands a great gray stone monument, set there by the government to mark the line between the United States and Mexico.

To the south, several hundred miles distant, stretches the long Sea of Cortez, as the conquerors of ancient Mexico once called the Gulf of California. Beyond the Sea of Cortez is the long and rock-bound reach of the west coast of Mexico. Then a group of little Central American republics; then Colombia, Peru and so on, till at last Patagonia points away like a huge giant's finger straight toward the South Pole.

But I must bear in mind that I set out in this story to tell about "The Bear-Slayer of San Diego," and the South Pole is a long way from the subject in hand.

I have spoken of San Diego as one of the great new cities, and great it is, but altogether new it certainly is not, for it was founded by a Spanish missionary, known as Father Junipero, more than one hundred years ago.

These old Spanish missionaries were great men in their day; brave, patient and very self-sacrificing in their attempts to settle the wild countries and civilize the Indians.

This Father Junipero walked all the way from the City of Mexico to San Diego, although he was more than fifty years old; and finally, after he had spent nearly a quarter of a century in founding missions up and down the coast of California, he walked all the way back to Mexico, where he died.

When it is added that he was a lame man, that he was more than threescore and ten years of age, and that he traveled all the distance on this last journey on foot and alone, with neither arms nor provisions, trusting himself entirely to Providence, one can hardly fail to remember his name and speak it with respect.

This new city, San Diego, with its most salubrious clime,

is set all over and about with waving green palms, with golden oranges, red pomegranates, great heavy bunches of green and golden bananas, and silver-laden olive orchards. The leaf of the olive is of the same soft gray as the breast of the dove. As if the dove and the olive branch had in some sort kept companionship ever since the days of the deluge.

San Diego is nearly ten miles broad, with its base resting against the warm, still waters of the Pacific Ocean. The most populous part of the city is to the south, toward Mexico. Then comes the middle part of San Diego City. This is called "the old town," and here it was that Father Junipero planted some palm trees that stand to this day— so tall that they almost seem to be dusting the stars with their splendid plumes.

Here also you see a great many old adobe houses in ruins, old forts, churches, fortresses, barracks, built by the Mexicans nearly a century ago, when Spain possessed California, and her gaudy banner floated from Oregon to the Isthmus of Darien.

The first old mission is a little farther on up the coast, and the new college, known as the San Diego College of Letters, is still farther on up the warm sea bank. San Francisco lies several hundred miles on up the coast beyond Los Angeles. Then comes Oregon, then Washington, one of the newest States, and then Canada, then Alaska, and at last the North Pole, which, by the way, is almost as far as the South Pole from my subject: The Bear-Slayer of San Diego.

He was a little Aztec Indian, brown as a berry, slim and slender, very silent, very polite and not at all strong.

It was said that he had Spanish blood in his veins, but it did not show through his tawny skin. It is to be conceded, however, that he had all the politeness and serene dignity of the proudest Spanish don in the land.

He was now, by the kind favor of those good ladies who had heard of his daring address in killing the bear with his

61

knife, a student of the San Diego College of Letters, where there were several hundred other boys of all grades and ages, from almost all parts of the earth.

A good many boys came here from Boston and other eastern cities to escape the rigors of winter. I remember one boy in particular from Philadelphia. He was a small boy with a big nose, very bright and very brave. He was not a friend of the little Aztec Indian, the Bear-Slayer of San Diego. The name of this boy from Philadelphia was Peterson; the Boston boys called him Bill Peterson. His name, perhaps, was William P. Peterson; William Penn Peterson, most likely. But this is merely detail, and can make but little difference in the main facts of the case.

As I said before, these college grounds are on the outer edge of the city. The ocean shuts out the world on the west, but the huge chaparral hills roll in on the east, and out of these hills the jackrabbits come down in perfect avalanches at night, and devour almost everything that grows.

Wolves howl from these hills of chaparral at night by hundreds, but they are only little bits of shaggy, gray coyotes and do little or no harm in comparison with the innumerable rabbits. For these big fellows, on their long, bent legs, and with ears like those of a donkey, can cut down with their teeth a young orchard almost in a single night.

The new college, of course, had new grounds, new bananas, oranges, olives, all things, indeed, that wealth and good taste could contribute in this warm, sweet soil. But the rabbits! You could not build a fence so high that they would not leap over it.

"They are a sort of Jumbo grasshopper," said the smart boy from Boston.

The head gardener of the college campus and environment grew desperate.

"Look here, sir," he said to the president, "these big-eared fellows are lazy and audacious things. Why can't they live up in the chaparral, as they did before we came here to plant trees and try to make the world beautiful? Now, either these jackrabbits must go or we must go."

"Very well," answered the president. "Offer a reward for their ears and let the boys destroy them."

"How much reward can I offer?"

"Five cents apiece, I think, would do," answered the head of the college, as he passed on up the great stone steps to his study.

The gardener got the boys together that evening and said, "I will give you five cents apiece for the ears of these dreadful rabbits."

"That makes ten cents for each rabbit, for each rabbit has two ears!" shouted the smart boy from Boston.

Before the dumfounded gardener could protest, the boys had broken into shouts of enthusiasm, and were running away in squads and in couples to borrow, buy or beg firearms for their work.

The smart boy from Boston, however, with an eye to big profits and a long job, went straight to the express office, and sent all the way to the East for a costly and first-class shotgun.

The little brown Aztec Indian did nothing of that sort; he kept by himself, kept his own counsel, and so far as any of the boys could find out, paid no attention to the proffered reward for scalps.

Bill Peterson borrowed his older brother's gun and brought in two rabbits the next day. The Boston boy, with an eye wide open to future profits to himself, went with Peterson to the head gardener, and holding up first one dead jackrabbit by the ear, and then the other, coolly and deliberately counted off four ears.

The gardener grudgingly counted out two dimes, and then, with a grunt of satisfaction, carried away the two big rabbits by their long hind legs.

As the weeks wore by, several other dead rabbits were reported, and despite the grumbling of the head gardener, the tumultuous and merry students had quite a revenue, and their hopes for the future were high, especially when that artillery should arrive from Boston!

Meantime, the little brown Aztec boy had done nothing at all. However, when Friday afternoon came, he earnestly begged, and finally obtained, leave to go down to his home at Tia Juana. He wanted very much to see his Mexican mother and his six little Mexican brothers, and his sixty, more or less, little Mexican cousins.

But lo! on Saturday morning, bright and early, back came the little Bear-Slayer, as he was called by the boys, and at his heels came toddling and tumbling not only his six half-naked little brown brothers, but dozens of his cousins.

Each carried a bundle on his back. These bundles were long, finely woven bird-nets, and these nets were made of the fiber of the misnamed century plant, the agave.

This queer looking line of barefooted, bareheaded, diminutive beings, headed by the silent little Aztec, hastily dispersed itself along the outer edge of the grounds next to the chaparral abode of the jackrabbits, and then, while grave professors leaned from their windows, and a hundred curious white boys looked on, these little brown fellows fastened all their long bird-nets together, and stretched two wide wings out and up the hill.

Very quiet but very quick they were, and when all the nets had been unwound and stretched out in a great letter V far up the hill, it was seen that each brown boy had a long, heavy manzanita wood club in his hand.

Suddenly and silently as they had come they all disappeared up and over the hills beyond, and in the dense black chaparral. Where had they gone and what did all this mystery mean? One, two, three hours! What had become of this strange little army of silent brown boys?

Another hour passed. Not a boy, not a sign, not a sound. What did it all mean?

Suddenly, down came a rabbit, jumping high in the air, his huge ears flapping forward and back, as if they had wilted in the hot sun.

Then another rabbit, then another! Then ten, twenty, forty, fifty, five hundred, a thousand, all jumping over each other and upon each other, and against the nets, with their long legs thrust through the meshes, and wriggling and struggling till the nets shook as in a gale.

Then came the long lines of half-naked brown boys tumbling down after them out of the brush, and striking right and left, up and down, with their clubs.

In less than ten minutes from the time they came out of the brush, the little fellows had laid down their clubs and were dragging the game together.

The grave professors shook their hats and handkerchiefs, and shouted with delight from their windows overhead, and all the white boys danced about, wild with excitement.

That is, all but one or two. The boy from Boston said savagely to the little Aztec, as he stood directing the counting of the ears, "You're a brigand! You're the black brigand of San Diego City, and I can whip you!"

The brigand said nothing, but kept on with his work.

In a little time the president and head gardener came forward, and roughly estimated that about one thousand of the pests had been destroyed. Then the kindly president went to the bank and brought out one hundred silver dollars, which he handed to the little Bear-Slayer of San Diego in a cotton handkerchief.

The poor, timid little fellow's lips quivered. He had never seen so much money in all his life. He held his head down in silence for a long time and seemed to be thinking hard. His half-naked little brothers and cousins grouped about and seemed to be waiting for a share of the money.

65

The boy's schoolmates also crowded around, just as boys will, but they did not want any of the silver, and I am sure that all, save only one or two, were very glad because of his good luck.

Finally, lifting up his head and looking about the crowd of his school-fellows, he said, "Now, look here; I want every one of you to take a dollar apiece, and I will take what is left." He laid the handkerchief that held the silver dollars down on the grass and spread it wide open.

Hastily but orderly, his schoolmates began to take up the silver, his own little brown fellows timidly holding back. Then one of the white boys who had hastily helped himself saw, after a time, that the bottom was almost reached, and, with the remark that he was half ashamed of himself for taking it, he quietly put his dollar back. Then all the others, fine, impulsive fellows who had hardly thought what they were about at first, did the same; and then the little brown boys came forward. They kept coming and kept taking, till there was not much but his handkerchief left. One of the professors then took a piece of gold from his pocket and gave it to the little Bear-Slayer. The boy was so glad that tears came into his eyes and he turned to go.

"See here! I'm sorry for what I said. Yes, I am. I ought to be ashamed, and I am ashamed."

It was the smart boy from Boston who had been looking on all this time, and who now came forward with his hand held out.

"See here!" he said. "I've got a forty-dollar shotgun to give away, and I want you to have it. Yes, I do. There's my hand on it. Take my hand, and you shall have the gun just as soon as it gets here."

The two shook hands, and the boys all shouted with delight; and on the very next Saturday one of these two boys went out hunting quail with a fine shotgun on his shoulder.

It was the silent little hero, The Bear-Slayer of San Diego.

XIII

BEARS OF THE NORTH

NEARLY FORTY YEARS AGO, when down from the Indian country to sell some skins in San Francisco, I saw a great commotion around a big ship in the bay, and was told that a Polar bear had been discovered floating on an iceberg in the Arctic, and had been taken alive by the ship's crew.

I went out in a boat, and on boarding the ship, just down from Alaska with a cargo of ice, I saw the most beautiful specimen of the bear family I ever beheld. A long body and neck, short legs, small head, cream-white and clean as snow, this enormous creature stood before us on the deck, as docile as a lamb. This is as near as ever I came to encountering the Polar bear, although I have lived in the Arctic and have more than one trophy of the bear family from the land of everlasting snows.

Bear are very plenty in Alaska and the Klondike country, and they are, perhaps, a bit more ferocious than in California, for I have seen more than one man hobbling about the Klondike mines on one leg, having lost the other in an argument with bear.

As a rule, the flesh is not good, here, in the salmon season, for the bear is in all lands a famous fisherman. He sits by the river and, while you may think he is asleep, he thrusts his paw deep down, and, quick as wink, he lands a huge salmon in his bunch of long, hooded claws.

A friend and I watched a bear fishing for hours on the Yukon, trying to learn his habits. I left my friend, finally, and went to camp to cook supper. Then, it seems, my friend shot him, for his skin, I think. Thinking the bear dead, he called to me and went up to the bear, knife in hand. But the bear rose up when he felt the knife, caught the man in his arms and they rolled in the river together. The poor man

67

could not get away. When we recovered his body far down the river next day, the bear still held him in her arms. She was a long, slim cinnamon, said to be the most savage fighter in that region.

All the bear of the far north seem to me to have longer bodies and shorter legs than in other lands. The black bear (there are three kinds of them) are bow-legged, I think; at least they "toe in," walk as an Indian walks, and even step one foot over the other when taking their time on the trail. We cultivated the acquaintance of a black bear for some months, on the Klondike, in the winter of '97–'98, and had a good chance to learn his habits. He was a persistent robber and very cunning. He would eat anything he could get, which was not much, of course, and when he could not get anything thrown to him from a door he would go and tear down a stump and eat ants. I don't know why he did not hibernate, as other bears in that region do. He may have been a sort of crank. No one who knew about him, or who had been in camp long, would hurt him; but a crowd of strangers, passing up the trail near our Klondike cabin, saw him, and as he did not try to get away he was soon dead. He weighed four hundred pounds, and they sold him where he lay for one dollar a pound.

I fell in with a famous bear-hunter, a few miles up from the mouth of the Klondike early in September, before the snow fell, and with him made a short hunt. He has wonderful bear sense. He has but one eye and but one side of a face, the rest of him having been knocked off by the slash of a bear's paw. He is known as Bear Bill.

The moss is very deep and thick and elastic in that region, so that no tracks are made except in a worn trail. But Bill saw where a bit of moss had been disturbed away up on a mountain side, and he sat right down and turned his one eye and all his bear sense to the solution of the mystery.

At last he decided that a bear had been gathering moss for

In a second, the big brown fellow was on his hind feet.

a bed. Then he went close up under a cliff of rocks and in a few minutes was peering and pointing down into a sunken place in the earth. And behold, we could see the moss move! A bear had covered himself up and was waiting to be snowed under. Bill walked all around the spot, then took position on a higher place and shouted to the bear to come out. The bear did not move. Then he got me to throw some rocks. No response. Then Bill fired his Winchester down into the moss. In a second the big brown fellow was on his hind feet looking us full in the face and blinking his little black eyes as if trying to make us out. Bill dropped him at once, with a bullet in his brain.

I greatly regret that I never had the good fortune to encounter a Polar bear, so that I might be able to tell you more about him and his habits; for men of science and writers of books are not bear-hunters, as a rule, and so real information about this white robber-monk of the cold, blue north is meager indeed. But here is what the most eminent English authority says about the nature and habits of this one bear that I have not shaken hands with, or encountered in some sort of way on his native heath:

"The great white bear of the Arctic regions—the 'Nennok' of the Eskimo—is the largest as well as one of the best known of the whole family. It is a gigantic animal, often attaining a length of nearly nine feet and is proportionally strong and fierce. It is found over the whole of Greenland; but its numbers seem to be on the decrease. It is distinguished from other bears by its narrow head, its flat forehead in a line with its prolonged muzzle, its short ears and long neck. It is of a light, creamy color, rarely pure white, except when young, hence the Scottish whalers call it the 'brounie' and sometimes the 'farmer,' from its very agricultural appearance as it stalks leisurely over the furrowed fields of ice. Its principal food consists of seals, which it persecutes most indefatigably; but it is somewhat omnivorous in its diet, and will often clear an islet of eider duck eggs in the course of a few hours. I once saw it watch a seal for half a day, the seal continually escaping, just as the bear was about putting his foot on it, at the atluk (or escape hole) in the ice. Finally, it tried to circumvent its prey in another maneuver. It swam off to a distance, and when the seal was again half asleep at its atluk, the bear swam under the ice, with a view to cut off its retreat. It failed, however, and the seal finally escaped. The rage of the animal was boundless; it moaned hideously, tossing the snow in the air, and at last trotted off in a most indignant state of mind.

"Being so fond of seal-flesh, the Polar bear often proves a great nuisance to seal-hunters, whose occupation he naturally regards as a catering to his wants. He is also glad of the whale carcasses often found floating in the Arctic seas, and travelers have seen as many as twenty bears busily discussing the huge body of a dead whalebone whale.

"As the Polar bear is able to obtain food all through the Arctic winter, there is not the same necessity, as in the case of the vegetable-eating bears, for hibernating. In fact, the males and young females roam about through the whole winter, and only the older females retire for the season. These—according to the Eskimo account, quoted by Captain Lyon—are very fat at the commencement of winter, and on the first fall of snow lie down and allow themselves to be covered, or else dig a cave in a drift, and then go to sleep until the spring, when the cubs are born. By this time the animal's heat has melted the snow for a considerable distance, so that there is plenty of room for the young ones, who tumble about at their ease and get fat at the expense of their parent, who, after her long abstinence, becomes gradually very thin and weak. The whole family leave their abode of snow when the sun is strong enough to partially melt its roof."

The Polar bear is regularly hunted with dogs by the Eskimo. The following extract gives an account of their mode of procedure:

"Let us suppose a bear scented out at the base of an iceberg. The Eskimo examines the track with sagacious care, to determine its age and direction, and the speed with which the animal was moving when he passed along. The dogs are set upon the trail, and the hunter courses over the ice in silence. As he turns the angle of the berg his game is in view before him, stalking along, probably, with quiet march, sometimes snuffing the air suspiciously, but making, nevertheless, for a nest of broken hummocks. The dogs spring forward, opening a wild, wolfish yell, the driver shrieking *Nannook! Nannook!* and all straining every nerve in pursuit.

"The bear rises on his haunches, then starts off at full speed. The hunter, as he runs, leaning over his sledge, seizes the traces of a couple of his dogs and liberates them from their burthen. It is the work of a minute, for the motion is not checked, and the remaining dogs rush on with apparent ease. Now, pressed more severely, the bear makes for an iceberg, and stands at bay, while his two foremost pursuers halt at a short distance and await the arrival of the hunter. At this moment the whole pack are liberated; the hunter grasps his lance, and, tumbling through the snow and ice, prepares for the encounter.

"If there be two hunters, the bear is killed easily; for one makes a feint of thrusting the spear at the right side, and, as the animal turns with his arms toward the threatened attack, the left is unprotected and receives the death wound."

73

XIV

MONNEHAN, THE GREAT BEAR-HUNTER

HE WORE A TALL SILK HAT, the first one I had ever seen, not at all the equipment of "a mighty hunter before the Lord." Phineas Monnehan, Esq., late of some castle (I forget the name now), County of Cork, Ireland, made mighty pretension to great estates and titles at home, but greatest of all his claims was that of "a mighty hunter."

Clearly he had been simply a schoolmaster at home, and had picked up all his knowledge of wild beasts from books. He had very impressive manners and had come to Oregon with an eye to political promotion, for he more than once hinted to my quiet Quaker father, on whose hospitality he had fastened himself, that he would not at all dislike going to Congress, and would even consent to act as Governor of this far-off and half-savage land known as Oregon. But, as observed a time or two before, Monnehan most of all things desired the name and the renown, like Nimrod, the builder of Babylon, of "a mighty hunter."

He had brought no firearms with him, nor was my father at all fond of guns, but finally we three little boys, my brother John, two years older than I, my brother James, two years younger, and myself, had a gun between us. So with this gun, Monnehan, under his tall hat, a pipe in his teeth and a tremendously heavy stick in his left hand would wander about under the oaks, not too far away from the house, all the working hours of the day. Not that he ever killed anything. In truth, I do not now recall that he ever once fired off the gun. But he got away from work, all the same, and a mighty hunter was Monnehan.

He carried this club and kept it swinging and sweeping in a semicircle along before him all the time because of the

incredible number of rattlesnakes that infested our portion
of Oregon in those early days. I shall never forget the terror
in this brave stranger's face when he first found out that all
the grass on all our grounds was literally alive with snakes.
But he had found a good place to stay, and he was not going
to be driven out by snakes.

You see, we lived next to a mountain or steep stony hill
known as Rattlesnake Butte, and in the ledges of limestone
rock here the rattlesnakes hibernated by thousands. In the
spring they would crawl out of the cracks in the cliffs, and
that was the beginning of the end of rattlesnakes in Oregon.
It was awful!

But we had a neighbor by the name of Wilkins, an old man
now, and a recent candidate for Governor of Oregon, who
was equal to the occasion. He sent back to the States and
had some black, bristly, razorbacked hogs brought out to
Oregon. These hogs ate the rattlesnakes. But we must get
on with the bear story; for this man Monnehan, who came
to us the year the black, razorbacked hogs came, was, as I
may have said before, "a mighty hunter."

The great high hills back of our house, black and wild and
woody, were full of bear. There were several kinds of bear
there in those days.

"How big is this 'ere brown bear, Squire?" asked Monnehan.

"Well," answered my father, "almost as big as a small
sawmill when in active operation."

"Oi think Oi'll confine me operations, for this hunting
sayson, to the smaller spacies o' bear," said Mr. Monnehan,
as he arose with a thoughtful face and laid his pipe on the
mantelpiece.

A few mornings later you would have thought, on looking
at our porch, that a very large negro from a very muddy
place had been walking barefooted up and down the length
of it. This was not a big bear by the sign, only a small black

cub; but we got the gun out, cleaned and loaded it, and by high noon we three little boys, my father and Monnehan, the mighty hunter, were on the track of that little black bear. We had gone back up the narrow canyon with its one little clump of dense woods that lay back of our house and reached up toward the big black hills.

Monnehan took the gun and his big club and went along up and around above the edge of the brush. My father took the pitchfork and my younger brother James kept on the ridge above the brush on the other side of the canyon, while my older brother John and myself were directed to come on a little later, after Mr. Monnehan had got himself in position to do his deadly work, and, if possible, drive the terrible beast within range of his fatal rifle.

Slowly and cautiously my brother and I came on, beating the brush and the tall rye grass. As we advanced up the canyon, Mr. Monnehan was dimly visible on the high ridge to the right, and father now and then was to be seen with little brother and his pitchfork to the left. Suddenly there was such a shout as almost shook the walls of the canyon about our ears. It was the voice of Monnehan calling from the high ridge close above the clump of dense wood; and it was a wild and a desperate and a continuous howl too. At last we could make out these words:

"Oi've thrade the bear! Oi've thrade the bear! Oi've thrade the bear!"

Down the steep walls came father like an avalanche, trailing his pitchfork in one hand and half dragging little brother James with the other.

"Run, boys, run! right up the hill! He's got him treed, he's got him treed! Keep around the bush and go right up the hill, fast as you can. He's got him treed, he's got him treed! Hurrah for Monnehan, at last! He's got him treed, he's got him treed!"

Out of breath from running, my father sat down at the

Mr. Monnehan, club in hand, was ready for the raging bear.

foot of the steep wall of the canyon below Monnehan and we boys clambered on up the grassy slope like goats.

Meantime, Monnehan kept shouting wildly and fearfully as before. Such lungs as Monnehan had! A mighty hunter was Monnehan. At last we got on the ridge up among the scattering and storm-bent and low-boughed oaks; breathless and nearly dead from exhaustion.

"Here, byes, here!"

We looked up the hill a little ahead of us from where the voice came, and there, straddled across the leaning bough of a broad oak tree hung Monnehan, the mighty hunter. His hat was on the ground underneath him, his club was still in his daring hand, but his gun was in the grass a hundred yards away.

"Here, boys, right up here. Come up here an' get a look at 'im! Thot's vaght Oi got up 'ere fur, to get a good look at 'im! Right up now, byes, an' get a good look at 'im! Look out fur me hat there!"

My brother hastily ran and got and handed me the gun and instantly was up the tree along with Monnehan, peering forward and back, left and right, everywhere. But no sign, no sound or scent of any bear anywhere.

By this time my father had arrived with his pitchfork and a very tired little boy. He sat down on the grass, and, wearily wiping his forehead, he said to Monnehan,

"Mr. Monnehan, how big was the bear that you saw?"

"Well, now, Squire, upon the sowl o' me, he was fully the size of a very extraordinary black dog," answered Mr. Monnehan, as he descended and came and stood close to my father, as if to defend him with his club. Father rose soon after and, with just the least tinge of impatience and vexation in his voice, said to brother John and me,

"Boys, go up and around the thicket with your gun and beat the bush down the canyon as you come down. Mr. Monnehan and I will drop down to the bottom of the can-

79

yon here between the woods and the house and catch him as he comes out."

Brother and I were greatly cheered at this; for it was evident that father had faith that we would find the bear yet. And believing that the fun was not over, we, tired as we were, bounded forward and on and up and around the head of the canyon with swift feet and beating hearts. Here we separated, and each taking a half of the dense copse of wood and keeping within hailing distance, we hastily descended through the steep tangle of grapevine, wild hops, wild gourdvines and all sorts of things, shouting and yelling as we went. But no bear or sign of bear as yet.

We were near the edge of the brush. I could see, from a little naked hillock in the copse where I paused to take breath, my father with his pitchfork standing close to the cow path below the brush, while a little further away and a little closer to the house stood Mr. Monnehan, club in hand and ready for the raging bear.

Suddenly I heard the brush break and crackle over in the direction of my brother. I dropped on my knee and cocked my gun. I got a glimpse of something black tearing through the brush like a streak, but did not fire.

Then I heard my brother shout, and I thought I heard him laugh too. Just then there burst out of the thicket and on past my father and his pitchfork a little black, razor-backed sow, followed by five black, squealing pigs! Monnehan's bear!